Poetry Stu

Songs of Ourselves \ ⌐, ⌐art 4

CIE IGCSE Literature in English 0475
CIE IGCSE (9-1) Literature in English 0992
Cambridge O level English Literature 2010
for examination in 2023, 2024 and 2025

Contents

Introduction

This guide is intended to support students working towards CIE IGCSE 0475 and 0992 and Cambridge O level English Literature 2010. There are 15 poems set for Paper 1 Poetry and Prose.

How to use this guide

Ideally this guide will support your in-class study of the poems, adding to the ideas and notes given to you by your teacher. But it can also be used as a complete independent study course if necessary.

- Read the notes with a copy of the text and a pen – be ready to annotate the poems!
- Read the poem carefully before, during and after reading the notes.
- Always get the 'story' of the poem clear in your mind before you get down to the fine detail of form, structure and language. *The story of the poem* sections should help with this.
- Ensure you can describe particular aspects of poetic technique (form, structure and language) in terms of their effect on the reader and their creation of meaning. It's not enough to spot a technique – you need to link it to meaning.
- Find an adult with whom you can discuss the poem; try out some of the *Talking points*, making sure you pin your answers to words and phrases from the poems.
- Pay particular attention to the italicised vocabulary in the *Tone* sections – having a range of words to describe tone is a good way to improve the sensitivity of your responses to poetry. Check you can match these tone words to particular quotes from the poems.
- *Style focus* sections have been added in a couple of places so that you can see how techniques and ideas can be brought together in focused discussion about a particular aspect of the poem.

The City Planners by Margaret Atwood

Now in her 80s, Atwood wrote this political, critical and cautionary poem back in the 1960s when she was about 25. Even as a young writer, it seems, she was preoccupied with the environment and the danger of authorities whose control over human lives borders on totalitarian. The major thrust of this poem is her intense dislike or distrust of the order created by the City Planners – the people who design suburban spaces and impose conformity on human populations.

The story of the poem

The speaker is 'cruising' a residential or suburban area and is offended by its orderly, clean, controlled appearance. But the speaker spots some small signs of imperfections and goes on to suggest that these are hints of what lies beneath the surface – the 'future cracks' that will eventually lead to the whole neighbourhood collapsing: slowly, chaos and nature will break through. The final three stanzas are a direct comment on the City Planners of the poem's title - the way they operate blindly and without co-ordination, 'guessing' and trying ineffectually to impose order.

The narrative, such as it is, is very slight. Atwood uses the first person plural ('us' in line 3 and 'our' in 8) but the poem has no characters and the focus is on describing a setting, not creating a story.

Form and structure

Written in seven uneven length stanzas and with very little rhyme, you could argue that the form of this poem celebrates chaos and a refusal to conform to expectations, rules and rigid structures. Free verse of this kind is not unusual for contemporary poems, but Atwood seems to go further than some poets in the way she uses punctuation unconventionally – the colon after 'certain things' in stanza two, for example. That stanza in particular seems quite messy, and its untidiness spills over into stanza three. All this reflects what she is discussing – the cracks in the orderly veneer of the suburban streets that will eventually result in nature taking over what humans have created. Atwood intentionally creates a poem that seems out of control at times.

If you look more closely, however, you can see that the poem falls into three parts beginning 'Cruising', 'But' and 'That is where'. So the structure is perhaps as follows: situation, disruption, problem. This adds to the didactic feeling of the poem – the sense that Atwood is presenting an argument and offering a warning to us. You should also notice how the poem is structured so that it moves from the local (stanzas one and two) to the global (stanza four), making it so much more than an observation on boring, bland city planning.

Another interesting way to view structure is to compare the beginning – 'August sunlight' – with the ending – 'a bland madness of snows'. The degeneration in the weather sounds an ominous, warning note, linked perhaps to ideas about climate change. The poem begins with stability – 'houses in pedantic rows' - and ends in chaos – 'a bland madness of snows'.

Language features

- Metaphor – 'a plastic hose poised in a vicious/coil' is a rather hyperbolic image in stanza two that turns a garden hose into a dangerous snake. In stanza four there is a slightly extended metaphor where houses are 'capsized' and the ground on which they are built becomes 'the clay seas'. This metaphor evokes those disaster movies where the earth opens up and swallows buildings, but it's useful for Atwood to make it watery because she is able to link it to the reality of current climate change when she says this will be as 'gradual as glaciers/that right now nobody notices'. It also links subtly to those everyday metaphors about sinking ships and even disasters such as the sinking of Titanic (see Wider reading, below). The snow imagery of the final three stanzas includes one striking metaphor – the 'private blizzard' of the City Planners. Blizzards evoke ideas of confusion and blindness: are the City Planners blind to the truth of what they are doing? Are they floundering around aimlessly in their own private blizzard, oblivious to anyone else? The snow imagery as a whole – 'white vanishing air' and 'bland madness of snows' - works to suggest this idea of ignorance and futility; the City Planners sketch 'transitory lines' on the snow, but nothing they do is permanent or worthwhile, so their actions are a kind of madness.
- Simile – 'a splash of paint...surprising as a bruise' is a very vivid simile. On the face of it, it's just suggesting that a blob of paint where it shouldn't be is similar to a bruise discolouring a body. But it brings together very subtly the domain of suburban décor and the domain of human skin, implying that there is something human, natural and organic beneath the surface of this unrealistically perfect residential street.
- Symbolism – it's possible to read a lot of what Atwood writes as symbolic – for example, the 'dent in our car door' could be seen as representing the bumps and imperfections that make us human.

- Personification – it's a commonplace to see windows as the eyes of a house. In stanza two, 'the too-fixed stare of the wide windows' personifies the house as a human who has become de-animated, frozen into an unnatural stare. 'Too-fixed' is judgemental in tone.
- Ambiguity – 'sanities' on line four blends two distinct meanings – clean and free of madness (think sanitise and sane) – both stemming from the Latin *san* meaning health. Even more interesting is the use of 'discouraged' at the end of stanza one. As an adjective, this word personifies the grass as demoralised or fed up, suggesting (in a hyperbolic metaphor) that this element of nature is fed up with the way it is being cut and organised into neat, straight lines. Atwood seems to be offering the grass as an example of the way in which joy and life have been stifled in this street. But it's also possible to read 'discouraged' as implying that the grass has been discouraged from growing, that the City Planners don't actually want anything organic that risks disturbing their beautifully ordered environment. Grass is to be discouraged because it's messy. Both readings work; ambiguity enriches the poem.
- Juxtaposition (Irony and Paradox) – it's jarringly unexpected that what 'offends' the speaker in line three is the 'sanities' – things that are clean, neat, orderly and rational. This creates irony or paradox and it is moments like these that offer us a challenge as readers. You could say Atwood's use of irony challenges us to rethink our idea of what is normal or natural. The same thing happens at the end of the poem when she juxtaposes panic and order in 'the panic of suburb/order': panic and order can't logically co-exist but Atwood interprets the desire to order things and assume a veneer of control as a City Planner's response to panic.
- Sibilance – the poem opens with significant sibilance (repetition of 's' sounds) across the first seven lines. This could be a recreation of the hushed quietness of the sleepy, sunny Sunday, or it could be interpreted as quite sinister; sibilance works in both ways and they aren't in fact as opposite as they seem. You could say Atwood's use of sibilance evokes the sinister deceptiveness of the quiet Sunday setting. Sibilance is used again in stanza two – linking 'smell...spilt...sickness...garages..splash..surprising...bruise...plastic hose poised ...vicious'. Here it is definitely sinister!
- Lexical field – of order eg 'pedantic rows', 'levelness of surface', 'straight swath' (stanza one), 'even' (stanza two). Notice how this then gives way to a new lexical field – one to do with destruction, violence and pain eg 'spilt', 'splash', 'bruise', 'vicious' (stanza two), 'cracks' (stanza three), 'capsized' (stanza four). Throughout the poem there is a lexical set of madness and sanity eg 'sanities', 'rational' (stanza one), 'hysteria' (stanza two), 'insane' (stanza five), 'panic', 'madness' (stanza seven), suggesting this is a dominant theme for the poem.
- Onomatopoeia – in stanza one, 'shatter' and 'whine' are both onomatopoeic – the latter is part of Atwood's recreation of the soundscape. But this technique is not dominant or even particularly significant in this poem.
- Plosive alliteration – in common with many writers, Atwood uses plosive alliteration to create a slightly scornful tone. For example, in stanza one the 'pedantic rows' of 'planted' trees, and in stanza two the 'plastic hose poised'. The 'p' sounds are made at the front of the mouth with a small explosion of air (hence plosive) which can be used to imply scorn or rejection. You need to say the lines aloud to feel it for yourself.

If you get a chance to write about the language of this poem, be aware that through her creative and original choices (her imagery and ambiguity, for example), Atwood is demonstrating something about the beauty of the human imagination. You could argue that her highly individual poem is in stark contrast to the bland uniformity she describes in the suburban world envisaged by the City Planners.

Style focus: the creation of setting

Atwood uses a range of techniques to create a setting that is eerily quiet, perfectly ordered and strangely stifling. Opting for a Sunday in 'August sunlight', Atwood seems to have deliberately chosen a quiet, semi-religious, warm setting. However, its very perfection makes it sinister and sterile – not just clean but barren. Even the lawnmower – the only sound – has a 'rational whine', suggesting it is sensible. The sibilance of the first seven lines adds to this effect. Despite the presence of trees and grass, the setting feels unnatural: the trees are 'sanitary' - which is a very odd word to use for bark rooted in the dirt – and the grass is 'discouraged', suggesting it is both disillusioned and unwanted rather than lush. At the same time the roofs have a 'slant of avoidance to the hot sky' suggesting they have turned their back on nature. The setting is very reminiscent of towns in dystopian fiction – manicured to perfection by a totalitarian regime that aims to control everything to a bland conformity, ruling out any individuality or creativity.

Beneath the monotony of perfection, however, there are warning signs of the chaos to come – 'spilt oil', 'sickness lingering' and a 'splash of paint' – and at this point Atwood's poem segues into an apocalyptic vision which involves houses metaphorically 'capsized' and on a 'slide' into 'clay seas'. The setting suddenly becomes much less parochial (local) and much more global, with reference to 'glaciers' which are many miles away from 'these residential Sunday/streets'. The hyperbole of the images in this central part of the poem works to suggest both the insanity of humans (ie the City Planners) trying to impose conformity and control onto nature, and the dangers of future climate change.

Style focus: the depiction of the City Planners

Despite being referenced in the title, the City Planners themselves do not feature until stanza five. Immediately this suggests a level of anonymity – they are working behind the scenes and what we see (the residential street) is a product of their work. However, in stanza five they are described as having 'the insane faces of political conspirators' and Atwood picks up on the motif of sanity/madness, openly and ironically judging these creators of the 'sanities' as 'insane'. What's more, she portrays them as engaging in some kind of conspiracy or plot, a group of politicians scheming. Some people see the capitalisation of City Planners as portraying them as gods, ruling over 'unsurveyed territories'. At the same time, Atwood contradicts herself slightly by claiming they are 'scattered' and work alone 'concealed from each other,/each in his own private blizzard'. The imagery of snow evokes ideas of confusion, blindness and ignorance. She says they are 'guessing directions', 'sketch[ing]' and 'tracing' – three verbs which don't inspire confidence that they are doing anything meaningful or permanent. The depiction is entirely negative. Whether she uses the male pronoun 'his' to suggest they represent the patriarchy is debatable.

Themes and ideas

- Conformity – Atwood critiques human preference for order and control, suggesting that this ends in a 'bland madness of snows' – a metaphor that suggests both a whiteout and confusion – certainly not something to be welcomed.
- Madness – playing on the ambiguity of sanity (clean and freedom from madness), Atwood explores the irony that what appears sane (the clean, orderly, controlled suburban environment) is in fact irrational or mad because it denies the power of nature. You could say this is an example of irony. Ultimately, the actions of the City Planners are seen as insane as they are floundering around in a 'private blizzard' sketching 'transitory lines' onto 'vanishing air', creating a 'bland madness'.

- Humans and the environment – although we attempt to control our environment with 'planted sanitary trees' and our 'slant of avoidance to the hot sky', Atwood suggests there will be 'future cracks' and 'capsized' houses. The argument seems to be that nature will eventually reclaim her own. At the same time, however, Atwood alludes to climate change and the (irreversible) damage done by humans when she writes about the melting glaciers 'that right now nobody notices'. So the environment is presented as both vulnerable and powerful while humans are presented as guilty and deluded.
- Colonisation – not a dominant idea but the mention of 'unsurveyed territories' coming under the scrutiny of the City Planners evokes ideas of colonisation and political regimes which take over different lands. In the past, colonisation was often justified as a act of civilising. Atwood seems to see the City Planners in the same light: they are confident their ideas about controlling the environment are right, that they will bring order. History has a different story to tell about colonisation and some of the dangers it brought to indigenous cultures.
- Time and transience – linked to the above, this is not a dominant idea but at a couple of points in the poem there is a sense that human efforts are transient – in other words, not of permanent, lasting value – and that time will defeat humans. The City Planners sketch 'transitory lines' in something like a snowstorm – snow being a very shifting form, liable to melt and disappear.

Tone

This is difficult to pin down. On the one hand, you could argue that the speaker is *calm, curious* and *confident*. The creative imagery discussed above adds to this sense of someone who is in control of their emotions, exploring an idea carefully and confidently. The idea of a three part structure (see above) also adds to this. On the other hand, you could argue that the speaker is *angry* and *determined*, seen in the list-like series of observations and the critical, sometimes hyperbolic, language of the images. It could also be argued that she is *disillusioned* and *contemptuous* – scornful about the City Planners and about humanity in general, since humanity seems to be presented as compliant with the whole process of designing sterile suburban spaces. If you feel that Atwood is trying to warn us or teach us, then you could argue she has a *didactic* tone. Above all, the speaker sounds *mature* and *thoughtful*.

Talking points

Is Atwood deliberately exaggerating - misrepresenting the efforts of the City Planners as dangerous as well as misguided?

Does her exaggeration (hyperbole) undermine the argument or make it more striking, and therefore more effective?

Which images do you find most effective and why?

Practice questions

How does Atwood create strong feelings about the environment in *The City Planners*?

How does Atwood use words and images to striking effect in *The City Planners*?

Wider reading and extension tasks for interested students

The Convergence of the Twain by Thomas Hardy. This was written to mark the huge loss of life following the sinking of Titanic. You could compare the way Hardy writes about human pride and vanity in the face of powerful natural forces.

London by William Blake. This late eighteenth century poem describes the 'chartered' streets and river of England's capital city. You could compare the way Blake sees such regulation as curtailing the ability of humans to think and act for themselves.

The Handmaid's Tale by Margaret Atwood. This novel centres on a dystopian setting – Gilead – where human lives have been controlled by a totalitarian regime. You could explore the way Atwood shows the human struggle to retain any sense of identity and creativity when your sense of what is normal has been challenged.

The Planners by Boey Kim Cheng

Almost 30 years after Atwood published her poem *The City Planners*, Boey Kim Cheng produced his rather bleak poem *The Planners* with a very similar theme: the horrors of urban modernisation which create perfect facades but deny any sense of individuality. Both poems allude to climate change, but in *The Planners* there is much more emphasis on the scale and pace of relentless development, and no prospect that the environment will break through to disrupt the process. In that respect, it offers an even bleaker vision of the future – one in which poets, like residents, are numbed into submission, unable to 'bleed' their hearts and offer a protest.

Boey Kim Cheng was born in Singapore and subsequently moved to Australia. Although he does not name the city he describes in *The Planners,* it is widely thought that he is writing about Singapore, a city which has seen rapid modernisation. Efficient use of limited land has resulted in the building of skyscrapers and the destruction of many older dwellings.

The story of the poem

The speaker tells us about the work of the planners who have 'gridded' the spaces and filled them with buildings, roads and bridges, following a mathematical design. They are so relentless that nature (in the form of the sea and the skies) has surrendered and retreated. The second stanza gives a little more detail about the process whereby the past is erased or corrected: gaps are filled and everything is made shiny and new. Crucially, the planners have the power to numb people to the process so that they forget the past and are mesmerised by the new architecture. The speaker only speaks once of himself – 'But my heart would not bleed/poetry' – in an ambiguous last stanza which suggests that he cannot or will not be inspired by this brave new world.

Form and structure

The poem is written across three uneven length stanzas and in free verse, with no obvious rhyme scheme. This could be seen as a rebellion against the mathematical precision of the new 'gridded' spaces and 'perfect rows' described by the poem. You could say the form of the poem is in ironic contrast to the setting it depicts. One of the impacts of free verse is that it throws a lot of emphasis on the poet's word choices and other linking devices such as sound. There is a lot of subtlety in this poem if you look for it – and perhaps that is the whole point: Boey Kim Cheng wants the reader to value the individual quirkiness of the form and the search for treasures which are lost when everything is 'gleaming' and 'perfect'. So his poem resists the conformity he describes and celebrates individuality and creativity.

Some people might choose to see the jagged outline of the poem as a representation of the city skyline (although you need to turn the page through 90 degrees to get the effect and what is described in stanza two is 'perfect rows' rather than an uneven skyline – so this is not a certain reading).

Structurally, the second stanza reads like a development of the first – incorporating an extended metaphor of dentistry to give a clearer view of the perfection described in stanza one. The third is a complete departure – a personal response which is suddenly very emotive. This creates a dramatic shift in tone (see below) and acts as an abrupt full stop to the poem.

Language features

- Anaphora – the poem begins with the anaphora of 'They plan. They build.' – successive sentences that begin in the same way. Together with the simplicity of the sentences and the stops created by the caesurae (the punctuation), this creates a hugely impactful first line, with emphasis on the anonymous planners using the third person pronoun 'They'. The planners are unseen and unidentified, but very busy. The effect is quite sinister.

- Repetition and parallelism – as with the anaphora explored above, repetition creates emphasis and is seen elsewhere with 'will not stop' (stanza one and two). A similar effect is seen with parallel phrasing – 'The piling will not stop' and 'The drilling goes right through' (stanza two). Parallel phrasing creates rhythm and begins to add to the sense of relentlessness – the planners are driving their agenda just as they are driving piles and drills into the ground.

- Personification – 'the sea draws back' could be read as literal and might not immediately suggest personification but the subsequent line 'and the skies surrender' (stanza one) means that both sea and skies have been personified as combatants in a battle between nature and humans. It's a battle in which they have withdrawn and surrendered, given up, abandoned the fight. This is a particularly bleak moment in the poem.

- Extended metaphor – in stanza two there is an extended metaphor of dentistry with reference to 'dental dexterity', 'gaps', fillings of 'gold', 'perfect rows/of shining teeth', 'anaesthesia' and 'drilling'. The metaphor works: building shiny new blocks which are neatly aligned is rather like having your teeth straightened and whitened, or having a set of neat dental implants to create the perfect – albeit somewhat artificial - smile. And sometimes you have to be anaesthetised to numb the pain. The last reference to 'drilling' is particularly appropriate since it's a verb that relates directly to both building and dentistry. The extended metaphor also works on a more subtle level to position the planners as dentists; many people have a love-hate relationship with dentists and see them as people who inflict pain, working in a cold, sterile environment! All those emotions and ideas are brought to the fore through the extended metaphor.

- Lexical sets – apart from the extended metaphor of dentistry (see above), there is a clear lexical set related to architectural design and building –'build', 'gridded', 'buildings', 'alignment', 'bridges', 'mathematics', 'build' (stanza one), 'blocks', 'piling', 'drilling' (stanza two), 'blueprint' (stanza three). Interestingly, there is a positive vibe around these terms for the first six lines of stanza one – helped by the phrase 'grace of mathematics' since grace is a very positive abstract concept. The lexical choice of 'desired' adds to this sense of positivity. Later in the poem, the speaker suggests people have been numbed (anaesthetised) into accepting the building programme and the start of the poem seems to illustrate that. It's easy to be lulled into thinking this is going to be a positive poem about change. All that shifts, of course, with the ominous seventh line 'They build and will not stop'.

- Cacophony – an unpleasant collection of sounds is cacophonous – it can have a jarring effect and suggest that what is being described is unpleasant or dangerous. Boey Kim Cheng creates cacophony in stanza two with the plosive alliteration of 'dental dexterity' and the guttural 'g' sounds in 'gaps are plugged/with gleaming gold' (stanza two). Guttural refers to sounds made at the back of the throat.

- Euphony – the sibilance of 'Anaesthesia, amnesia, hypnosis' combines with the soft 'h' and 'm' sounds of 'They have the means./They have it all so it will not hurt,/so history is new again' (stanza two) to create a pleasant, lulling effect that directly contrasts with the early guttural sounds. This subtly lulls the reader just as anaesthesia would – it takes away the pain. You could say that the poet's patterning of sound reflects the process by which the city dwellers are lulled into accepting what may at first seem harsh.
- Sibilance – at the end of stanza one, when nature gives up, 'the sea draws back/and the skies surrender' is made more sinister through the use of sibilance.
- Tricolon – 'Anaesthesia, amnesia, hypnosis' is a powerful line in stanza two. The tricolon is progressive, meaning that one thing leads to another – people are first numbed (maybe stunned or overwhelmed) by the pace of development, then they forget about the past and what they have lost, undergoing a kind of collective amnesia. In the end, they are mesmerised (another term for hypnosis) by the 'gleaming gold' of the 'perfect rows'. The problem with hypnosis, though, is that it's an unreal state, artificially induced and separating us from our real selves and our real lives. Who wants to live in a permanent state of amnesia and hypnosis? It's a really powerful tricolon. It could be read as a list of the weapons in the planners' armoury – the tools or means by which they suppress or eliminate protest.
- Metaphor – aside from the personification and the extended metaphor (see above) there is a powerful metaphor in the final stanza: 'my heart would not bleed/poetry'. Bleeding carries connotations of a person's energy or life force pouring out and this works well as a metaphor for poetry: writing poems requires poets to give something of themselves, their passion, their emotions – all this is poured out onto the page. The metaphor is extended slightly when the speaker says 'Not a single drop/to stain the blueprint'. The use of the word 'stain' is interesting here – how could poetry stain the modernisation programme? Perhaps it is used ironically, in a mocking way: the speaker knows that poetry has the potential to bleed all over the work of the planners, to highlight the damage it is doing, to raise public consciousness about this violation of nature and history. But oddly, Boey Kim Cheng seems to be saying he cannot or will not do this. You'll have to make up your own mind about this enigmatic ending...
- Enjambment – this serves two key purposes in the poem. It can suggest the relentlessness of the planning process – the fact that it will not stop but spills over from line to line. You can see this in the first stanza (lines 3-6). It also serves to emphasise those lines that are end-stopped, like the emphatic 'They have the means.' and 'The piling will not stop.' in stanza two.

Themes and ideas

- Modernisation and urban development – this is the main theme of the poem and by the end it is clear that Boey Kim Cheng's speaker is not a fan. The lexis around logic and order in stanza one ('gridded', 'filled', 'alignment', 'mathematics') is initially positive but increasingly feels artificial, non-organic and exercised at a cost to humanity; the planners 'erase' the past and with it a rich cultural history – 'the fossils of last century'. The withdrawal and surrender of nature at the end of stanza one cements the feeling that the actions of the planners have resulted in something significant and unnatural. This is ultimately about humans exerting power and control over the environment (see below). Modernisation is presented as functional – 'meet at desired points' and 'linked by bridges' (stanza one) – but also relentless – 'They will not stop' – and ubiquitous (everywhere) – 'All gaps are plugged'.
- The erasure of history – there are four specific references to the past: 'They erase the flaws,/the blemishes of the past', 'so history is new again', 'The drilling goes right through/the fossils of last century' (stanza two) and 'the blueprint/of our past's tomorrow' (stanza three). Erasing history

has two strands: the loss of cultural inheritance and a collective amnesia or denial of the past. Both are implied in the poem. To erase blemishes may seem a good thing (like removing depictions of slavery from art galleries) but ultimately it is a denial of reality; humans have made mistakes in the past and maybe we need to see those mistakes to learn from them – they are part of our cultural identity. More significantly, however, 'blemishes' could be quirks – interesting but slightly uneven or ramshackle buildings with a fascinating history. One person's blemish is another person's treasure? The idea of history being 'new again' is deeply ironic; re-writing history is the stuff of dystopian fiction like George Orwell's *Nineteen Eighty-Four* (see Wider reading, below). The reference to drilling through 'the fossils of last century' is ambiguous. On the one hand, the building programme could be literally destroying what remains of the architecture from the past (the 'fossils') in an act of cultural vandalism. On the other hand, this could be a reference to a much wider environmental concern about the way modernisation has relied on fossil fuels, plundering the earth in order to feed the human need for energy.

- Time – the above themes relate closely to ideas about the passage of time. It's worth noting that the poem is written entirely in the present tense, creating a sense of immediacy: this is happening right now. The only exception is the enigmatic opening to the third stanza – 'But my heart would not bleed'. 'Would' is a modal verb that usually sets up a conditional tense in the past. So, the speaker seems to be saying his heart did not bleed, it would not bleed, it could not bleed poetry at the sight of all this modernisation. Perhaps, if we assume an autobiographical reading, Boey Kim Cheng is reflecting that this is something he could not write about while it was happening, while he was living in Singapore. But conditional tenses are often related to future events – so it's possible to read this line as meaning that if all this modernisation continues, his heart will not be able to bleed poetry. Perhaps he is suggesting that poets, like other citizens, can be anaesthetised into silence or left uninspired by ubiquitous modernity.

- Nature – there are minimal references to the natural world in the poem which feels like a deliberate act: nature has been squeezed out in the planners' vision for the urban spaces. The sea and the skies are personified at the end of stanza one as retreating from a battle with humans - 'Even the sea draws back/and the skies surrender' – with sinister sibilance adding to the idea of how harmful this might be. The reference to the 'fossils of last century' can be interpreted as the land preserving evidence from the past but now being plundered with 'drilling' that 'goes right through' – a violation of the land and its relics. Alternatively, as noted above, this could be seen as a reference to environmental concerns about the exploitation of the earth in search of fossil fuels. Whichever interpretation you prefer, the message is the same: humans are destroying nature.

- Power – the ideas above can also be considered under the theme of power – humans are exerting power over the natural world and over the past: 'They have the means' is a very sinister and emphatic line.

- Poetry as a political response – that puzzling final stanza won't go away! Perhaps Boey Kim Cheng is suggesting that poets should bleed (metaphorically) onto the blueprints of modernisation or any political actions that deny our past, our humanity or our responsibility to the environment. As well as suggesting a life force, blood also connotes violence and conflict. In the past his heart would not bleed but now he is able to engage with the issues – in the form of this poem.

Tone

Tone is a subjective judgement: it is perfectly possible to read a poem aloud in different ways, adopting a different tone. So you could argue that the speaker's tone here is initially *flat and emotionless* ('They plan. They build. All spaces are gridded'), but increasingly *cynical, ironic* and *angry* ('They have the means./They have it all'), moving into *despair* ('my heart would not bleed'). Some might argue that the speaker is *defiant* at the end – 'Not a single drop' – but that ending is ambiguous.

Talking points

What do you make of the final stanza? What do you think Boey Kim Cheng is suggesting when he says 'my heart would not bleed/poetry'?

Do you see this as an exaggerated response to a building programme? To what extent do you find yourself persuaded and emotionally engaged by the poem? Can you select parts of the poem which have most impact on you?

Practice Questions

How does Boey Kim Cheng use words and images to striking effect in *The Planners*?

How does Boey Kim Cheng create strong feelings about urban modernisation in *The Planners?*

Wider reading and extension tasks for interested students

London by William Blake. Written around 1792, Blake's vision of London is bleak, full of monotony and restriction. Compare the way he populates his miserable vision with people, unlike Boey Kim Cheng, but suggests similarly that the solution lies within us if we would only wake up to what is happening.

Nineteen Eighty-Four by George Orwell. This novel centres on a dystopian setting – Oceania – where human lives have been controlled by a totalitarian regime (led by Big Brother). You could explore the way Orwell shows the human struggle to retain any sense of what is true and good when your choices are so limited and the past is being over-written.

Brave New World by Aldous Huxley. Another dystopian fiction. You might be interested to see how Huxley envisages a society in which drugs - soma tablets - are used routinely by the populace to induce happiness and an unreal state of bliss. Everything in the World State is designed to eliminate pain or unpleasantness.

The Man with Night Sweats by Thom Gunn

This is the titular poem in a collection published around 1992, during the AIDS crisis when there was still no established cure for HIV infection. Although born in England, Thom Gunn had been living in the US for many years by that time and witnessed first-hand the devastating effects of HIV, particularly among the gay community. Gunn himself lived until 2004 but many of his close friends died and in this poem he imagines himself into the perspective of someone suffering with the symptoms of AIDS (night sweats being a common sign of developed infection), knowing that he will die. AIDS is never specifically mentioned, however, and at some distance from these events, the poem can be read as a more universal meditation on the failure of the body to protect us from illness and on the way in which young people often feel invincible – something that attracted comment during the more recent COVID 19 pandemic. So the poem is not autobiographical, but it is based on Gunn's observations and his imaginative engagement with the thoughts and experience of an anonymous dying man. It is written in the form of a *dramatic monologue*. Remember to use the term *speaker* or *persona* when writing about the first person voice – it is not Gunn speaking, but a character he has created.

The story of the poem

The speaker wakes up feeling cold. Previously asleep, enjoying his dreams, he is now drenched in sweat with the sheet clinging to him. He reflects on the fact that his body used to protect him and heal itself. In his youth he explored and adored taking risks, trusting his body to be strong. All these risks opened up the world to him. He returns to the present and is sad that his body has now let him down; his mind is racing with anxiety and his body is wrecked. He has to get up to change the bed but pauses, standing, to hug himself, trying to re-create that sense of a shield, despite realising that he can't protect himself from the avalanche of death/to come.
[illness]

Form and structure

Gunn is known for his use of tight, regular forms. In this poem he alternates four quatrains of alternating rhyme (abab) with four rhyming couplets (aa). The tight, very contained form could represent either entrapment – there is no escape from the illness entrapping the man – or an attempt to control emotion in the face of an illness that is out of control. The latter interpretation works with ideas about tone (see below): the tone of the poem is dignified, controlled, calm and completely devoid of any hysterical despair.

Looking more closely at the lines, however, although almost all have six syllables, in three of the final four stanzas some lines are given an additional syllable: 'I cannot but be sorry' and 'My mind reduced to hurry' in stanza five; 'Hugging my body to me' and 'The pains that will go through me' in stanza seven; and the final line 'To hold an avalanche off'. It could be argued that this reflects the way the disease is beginning to encroach on his dignity and his ability to retain control.

The poem is structured so that it moves from the present (stanza one) to the past (stanzas two to five) and then back into the present (stanzas six to eight) with a brief nod to the future at the end of stanza seven – 'The pains that will go through me'. The section in the past when the speaker reflects nostalgically on his youth is encased by stanzas focused on the present; his past is still a significant part of his life – it is not rejected but held in a hug of the present, cherished and valued. This is important when you come to consider Gunn's attitude to risk-taking. Contextually, some gay communities were criticised for behaviours which put them at risk of contracting HIV. In expressing no regret for his past, Gunn's speaker implicitly refutes these criticisms, and the structure as described here supports this reading.

Language features

- Motif – the metaphor of a 'shield' features three times – in stanzas two, five and seven. A shield is a barrier used to protect against enemy attack. Thinking about it like that takes us to a different age of knights in battle, but the idea here is that his 'flesh was its own shield' – the body healed itself, it didn't need any external help, it fought off the enemy (infection, illness) in a very natural way. Where the body was metaphorically (or literally) 'gashed', it healed itself. The full rhyme of 'shield' and 'healed' in stanza two adds to the sense that this is natural and satisfactory. What Gunn is referring to is the body's immune system. It is this, however, that breaks down under the attack of HIV infection – human immunodeficiency virus – which leads to AIDS – acquired immunodeficiency syndrome. It's possible to read 'gashed' more literally as a reference to the way skin is broken when drugs are injected, with needle-sharing a common cause of HIV infection. Later on, in stanza five, the metaphorical shield is 'cracked', just as the literal skin shield is broken by sores and infection. In stanza seven, 'shield' is used as a verb rather than a noun. This draws attention to the loss of a physical shield or barrier and the fact that the speaker is wholly reliant on his own actions now to create any kind of security. He has to hug himself in order to protect or shield himself against all that is happening to him. We could read into this not only the physical changes brought about by his illness, but perhaps also the hurtful prejudice that people with AIDS experienced in the late 80s. Using 'shield' as a verb draws attention to the speaker's isolation (see Themes, below). Reading this lengthy exploration should make you realise just how much meaning Gunn packs into this metaphor!

- Metaphor – the final line of the poem contains a powerful metaphor as death and disease is compared to 'an avalanche'. Death itself is never mentioned in the poem, but this metaphor evokes ideas of being overwhelmed or overtaken by an unstoppable onslaught of symptoms. Choosing an avalanche for this metaphor reflects Gunn's sense of an outside force that cannot be controlled by humans. It might also reflect the coldness of death and is sharply contrasted to the 'heat' of the first stanza.

- Ambiguity – the 'dreams of heat' in stanza one stand out because of the repeated elongated 'ee' sound (you can refer to this as *assonance* – a repeated vowel sound) and because they create ambiguity. Gunn might be referring quite literally to fever experienced during sleep, or to sexual dreams. 'Heat' connects the past (in terms of sexual encounters) and the present (night sweats) – the cause and the effect.

- Euphemism – nowhere in the poem does Gunn refer directly to sex or death. Instead he uses euphemism: sex is represented as 'heat' and 'residue' in stanza one and 'risk' in stanza three; death is 'an avalanche' in the final line.

- Euphony – poets often create strong but subtle sound effects so it's always worth reading poetry aloud in order to pick up on these. In this poem there is a marked contrast between the euphony – the pleasant sounds – of 'flesh...shield...healed' when the past is described and the hard sounds of 'cracked...reduced...reduced...wrecked' when the present is described. This is important for understanding the speaker's (and possibly Gunn's) feelings about the past – there is no regret (see Themes, below).

- Parallel phrases – in stanza five the lines 'My mind reduced to hurry' and 'My flesh reduced and wrecked' create a rhythmic parallelism that emphasises the way this disease impacts both mind and body – the whole of a person.

Themes and ideas

- Illness and mortality – the speaker is under no illusion about his illness and impending death. He acknowledges factually 'The pains that will go through me' in the poem's first use of future tense, and almost mocks his own actions in hugging himself 'As if hands were enough'. He knows that his body is failing him and the lexis of stanza five is central to this – 'cracked...wrecked'. The repetition of 'reduced' is also important – not only is his 'flesh reduced', reflecting the physical emaciation experienced by people with AIDS, but his mind is 'reduced to hurry', suggesting his thoughts are racing out of control with anxiety. In the next stanza he has 'to change the bed' which evokes ideas of a child bed-wetting – an infantilising image.

- Solitude and isolation – to me, this feels like the most important theme in the poem. Beginning with the first line 'I wake up cold', we have a strong sense of the speaker's isolation. The word 'cold' evokes ideas of being alone, lacking the warmth of love. At the end of that first stanza the image of a 'clinging sheet' is quite poignant – there is no human clinging to him, just a sheet. The personal pronouns throughout tell a story of isolation – they are all first person singular, apart from the gender neutral 'it' in reference to his own body. Even in recollections of the past, no other humans feature. So the first stanza foregrounds the idea of isolation, the pronouns throughout emphasise it and we return to the theme in the final three stanzas where the speaker has to 'change the bed' (there is no parent or carer to do this) and 'catch myself' – there is no-one else there to catch him, to save him. He has to hug himself because there is no other human comfort. So the poem is structured to begin and end with isolation.

- Nostalgia and youth – nostalgia is a sentimental or fond reflection on memories of the past. Look at stanza three: the speaker is entirely positive when he considers the past. It was a time when he 'grew' in confidence and 'explored', when he could 'trust' his body. It was a time when he 'adored' taking risks and becoming 'robust' or strong as a result. The enjambment in this stanza makes it pacy – it suggests his excitement as he recalls the past. Risk opened up 'A world of wonders'. The positive lexis in stanza three and four is overwhelming, given the context of his present situation. Youth is presented as a time for discovery, personal growth and empowerment, and he has no regrets. He is 'sorry' that the 'shield' of his body (his immune system) is 'cracked', but not sorry for the actions that led to this. There is a sense he may regret the way he will die, but not the way he lived.

Tone

Overall, Gunn's speaker is *wistful, nostalgic and sorrowful*. His nostalgia doesn't make him mournful however, and the voice of stanzas two to four is arguably *confident, strong and energised*, as he recalls his past fondly, *excited* by memory. The tone is slightly *fearful* at the end, but in general the tone of the poem is *dignified, controlled and calm*. There is no hysteria or despair.

Talking points

Is it the man's isolation or his illness that creates more pathos for you?

Does a poem's context matter? Do you read the poem differently knowing that it was written during the AIDS epidemic?

Practice Questions

Explore the ways in which Gunn makes *The Man with Night Sweats* so moving for you.

How does Gunn movingly convey illness and mortality in *The Man with Night Sweats*?

Wider reading and extension tasks for interested students

Lament by Thom Gunn is a much longer poem, written in the form of direct address to a dying man. The speaker accompanies his friend during death and afterwards reflects. You could compare the emotional pull of the two poems – one written from the perspective of the dying, the other written as an observation. You could also compare the way Gunn writes about the body.

Nothing Gold Can Stay by Robert Frost is a very short poem focused on the inevitability of death, viewed through the lens of nature. Compare the way the two poets write about death without naming it.

Dover Beach by Matthew Arnold is a Victorian poem about faith and doubt but it has the same elegiac tone as Gunn's poem. Can you isolate the words and images in the two poems that create this tone? Alternatively, research the context of *Dover Beach*: what connections can you make between the apparently very different times in which they were written?

Night Sweat by Robert Lowell

Robert Lowell is one of the twentieth century American confessional poets – meaning that his style is first person, autobiographical and intense, reading as though he were confessing his deepest thoughts and feelings to the reader. This poem was written in 1964 and can be described as *ars poetica* – a poem about the writing of poetry, or in this case, the failure to write poetry, because the subject matter is writer's block. Lowell suffered from bipolar disorder and the poem explores a nightmarish struggle to conquer self-doubt and restore balance to his life. It's a complex poem, dense in metaphor and fantastical, ambiguous images.

The story of the poem

The speaker describes his littered workroom and alludes to the fact that he has 'stalled' – he has writer's block. Instead of being in the cluttered workroom, he is 'living in a tidied room' where for ten nights he has experienced night sweats. The sweat is pouring off him and with it, a flood of ideas or poetic inspiration for his great work, his 'one writing', his 'life's fever'. But day to day life – 'the bias of existing' - is draining him and he can't convert this inspiration into finished work. Instead, he is blocked, inside him something is dying or has died. But suddenly his wife appears behind him bringing light which starts to make things better. He's still wet with the night sweat and all the struggle it represents, but her 'lightness alters everything' and she drags his depression off him with all her energy. He pities her that she must bear his burden like a turtle, but he pleads with her to help him.

Form and structure

Although the poem is one stanza, it is in fact a fusion of two sonnets. The first is quite Shakespearean in style – with an *abba cdcd efef gg* rhyme scheme – and written in just two or three sentences, with ideas tumbling onto the page, mimicking the chaos that he feels during his night sweat as his mind races. The second, beginning 'Behind me!', is more rogue (and therefore more interesting!) with its unusual rhyme scheme of *abab caac deffed*. The *sestet* (the final six lines) uses *chiasmus*, meaning that the rhymes are repeated in reverse – *def* then *fed*. This feels quite neat and satisfactory, which ties in with the poem's fragile sense of closure around the wife's ability to balance things for the speaker. It's certainly a lot more satisfying than the rhyming couplet of the first sonnet where 'urn' is paired with 'burn' in an intensely funereal moment!

But what is the significance of the sonnet form? Sonnets are traditionally love poems but are used much more fluidly now. However, the sonnet is tight and always imposes constraint on the writer – it's particularly difficult to write in English with only six rhymes as Lowell does in the second sonnet. This feels like intense poetic endeavour when the subject matter is the seeming impossibility of creating the great work – the 'one writing' – to which he aspires. So we could argue that Lowell is putting a lot of pressure on himself, trying to impose a discipline on his fluid and wilful imagination. Or that he feels trapped by his art.

And what about the double sonnet? One way to view this is to see the second sonnet as a surprise: the first confesses the anxiety he feels – a burning intense frustration. The poem could stop there, but instead, along comes his wife – 'Behind me! You!' – and she introduces light into his darkness, shoulders his burden, lightens his heavy load and gives him hope (see Juxtapositions, below). The second sonnet completes the first, just as she balances him, and implicitly it introduces the idea of love as she is his 'Dear Heart'. The difference in sonnet style might reflect a shift in his thinking.

The poem begins *in media res* and this, combined with the list and the multiple *caesurae*, means the reader shares some of the confusion and uncertainty being experienced by the speaker as his thoughts race.

Language features

- Motif of light – the poem has a recurring idea of light which is ambiguous since it refers not only to illumination and weightlessness (think of the opposites as dark and heavy), but it also has religious or spiritual connotations of inspiration and truth. It is the speaker's wife who brings light in all these forms. Initially her light 'lighten[s] my leaded eyelids' when the speaker's horses 'whinny for the soot of night' – in other words, she lightens up the dark and lifts a heavy weight off him. As a result of her arrival, his 'flesh and bedding' are 'washed with light' – just as in some religions water is used to wash a person, symbolising their purity as they see the light of truth. Her 'lightness alters everything' and yet she is the one who must be burdened with the weight of his struggle.
- Motif of child – there are three mentions of a child: 'always inside me is the child who died' (line 11), 'always inside me is his will to die' (line 12) and 'my child exploding into dynamite' (line 21). The child could be a metaphor for his unwritten work – it is dying before it can be born, it is resisting any efforts to live and then – after the wife appears – it is no longer soaked in sweat but powerful and strong.
- Juxtapositions/oppositions/binaries – the poem is patterned with these – look for light/dark, light/heavy, death/life, wet/dry, up/down, night/day. What does this mean? Essentially, it's about confusion and uncertainty, but also about the problem-solution structure of the poem (see above).
- Water imagery – the 'sweat' of the title opens the way for Lowell to use watery images both literally and metaphorically. So he feels the 'creeping damp' (line 4) of his sweat 'float' (line 5) over his PJs. Damp doesn't float, of course, but the verb choice begins to create a river image which is continued later when 'everything streams' (line 7) in his imagination. Meanwhile his 'head is wet' (line 6) and his 'life's fever is soaking in night sweat' (line 8). He doesn't have a literal fever so this seems to relate to the passion he feels for his work – that is his 'life's fever' and at the moment it is drowning. By way of contradiction, he says 'the bias of existing wrings us dry' (line 10), with dry being a common metaphor for writer's block. What all this amounts to is a sense that he can't win! He's drowning and he's dried up; maybe he has too many uncontrolled ideas and the sweat pours off him as an anxiety response. It's important not to worry about the lack of logic here; as with the imagery explored in detail below, the main thing is to feel his distress – he can't make sense of his situation and the somewhat muddled use of water imagery reflects this.
- Metaphor – 'my stalled equipment' in line 2 could be a metaphor for writer's block; more literally, his pen or typewriter has effectively stalled (as when an engine suddenly stops working) because he cannot think of what to write. Three lines from the end, 'troubled waters' is a metaphor for depression.
- Animal symbolism and zoomorphism – animals feature heavily in the second half of the poem. First the 'gray skulled horses' that 'whinny for the soot of night'. These seem nightmarish with their skeletal heads and their desire for night. They are the antithesis of the mythological horses which draw the sun up into the sky. As such they reflect the speaker's sense of his own heaviness, his association with darkness and the way he cannot escape the night without his wife's help. He also associates himself with spiders in a complex image (see below). Interestingly, spiders are used to symbolise creativity as they are versatile, industrious and produce intricate

designs. As with the horses, however, the speaker inverts this positivity, giving his spider a black web. The speaker's wife, by contrast, is a 'hare', an animal that features in a lot of myths and is thought to bring luck and protection. She is also a 'turtle' and a 'tortoise' – both of which carry a hard shell. With the turtle, the poet is drawing on the myth of the World's Turtle that features in several cultures, a creature which carries the world on its back. With the tortoise, although the image is similar, there is perhaps more subtlety as his wife is both the hare – energetic and lively – and the tortoise – steady and patient – from Aesop's fable. She is everything: a balanced individual. He, by contrast, seems dark, weak and heavy, reduced by the animal symbolism.

- Imagery – 'the black web of the spider's sack' is a complex image drawing on associations of darkness with depression and a web as a tangled form of entrapment. The spider's sack could be a referring to the egg sac carried by a spider – it contains a vast number of eggs and grows to a huge size relative to the spider's body. This could represent the speaker's ideas which he carries but over which there is a dark web of depressive thoughts, entangling and blocking the creative process. His wife 'tears the black web from the spider's sack', thus releasing him to be creative and give birth to his metaphorical spider poem babies. Alternatively, you might see the sack as housing all his darkest thoughts and self-doubt. It could be a metaphor for his subconscious mind. What do you think? The beauty of poetry is that we don't need to rely on a single reading of a complex image, but we do need to feel the weight of it: this is a heavy, serious depressive image.

- Sound effects – the liquid 'l' alliteration in 'light/lighten my leaded eyelids' (lines 15-16) and the aspirant 'h' alliteration of 'your heart hops and flutters like a hare' (line 24) make the second half of the poem feel much lighter than the first.

- Asyndeton – this refers to a list or series of clauses without conjunctions like 'and' or 'but'. We can also use the term *asyndetic listing* to describe what is happening at the start of the poem where the speaker lists 'Work-table, litter, books and standing lamp,/plain things, my stalled equipment, the old broom'. This list creates a cluttered feeling, much like the room it describes.

- Lexis of death – 'embalms' (line 6), 'died' (line 11), 'die' (line 12), 'urn' (line 13), 'burn' (line 14), 'skulled' and 'soot' (line 17). The frequency of these references creates a heavy mood.

- Anaphora – the repetition of 'always inside me..../always inside me' (lines 11 and 12) creates real emphasis – a driving, obsessive rhythm. The speaker feels trapped.

- Pronoun shift – notice the shift from multiple use of first person singular pronouns (I, me, my) to second person (you, your). For most of the poem the speaker is completely self-absorbed, but he ends with a strong focus on the addressee – the wife – and her role in restoring him.

- Ellipsis – on line 22 after 'my wife...' suggests that the very mention of her creates a pause, a moment after which he is able to move on in a more positive way, with hope for the future.

Themes and ideas

- The creative process - Lowell's poem suggests that writing is a struggle. Like his equipment he is 'stalled' (line 2), 'dry' (line 10) and mummified into a state of paralysis as 'Sweet salt embalms me' (line 6). This creates a strong sense of existential threat – as if he will die if he cannot produce his 'one writing' (line 9). The emphasis on 'one' is strong: he has 'one life' (line 9) in 'one body' (line 13) in 'one universe' (line 13) in which to produce his 'one writing'.

- Anxiety and depression - this is the product of his writer's block and is seen in the listing, the fragmented phrasing and the tumbling confusion of images, many of which can be read both literally and metaphorically. Particular features of his depression include the psychosomatic night sweats of the title (he isn't physically ill, but his mind is producing physical symptoms), 'the downward glide' (line 9), his 'leaded eyelids' (line 16), the 'black web' (line 23) and the 'troubled waters' (line 26).

- Relationships – this emerges in the second half of the poem as we see how important his wife is to him and his creative output. He seems dependent on her.

Tone

Lowell is *anxious* and seems *tortured*. His tone is one of *panic, anguish* and *frustration*. At the end he is *pleading* with the addressee but seems *hopeful* – able at last to look outside himself long enough to pity her ('Poor turtle') that she has to bear his burden.

Talking points

On balance, do you feel the night sweats are presented as destructive or productive? Do they represent his creative energy or his anxiety at his failure to write?

Is the complex imagery of the poem unique to his situation, or could it be applied to other forms of anxiety and depression? Which images do you find more relatable?

Practice Questions

How does Lowell vividly convey his anxiety in *Night Sweat*?

How does Lowell use words and images to striking effect in *Night Sweat*?

Wider reading and extension tasks for interested students

The Thought Fox by Ted Hughes is another *ars poetica*. Research the origins of this poem and compare the way the two writers have approached the difficulty of producing work during a writer's block. Can you find any connections between the poems?

Cozy Apologia by Rita Dove has a similar setting – the writer's workroom – and a similar focus on a relationship, but it is a very different poem. You could explore the way similar subject matter takes these two American poets in completely different directions. See if you can find any connections in the poetic techniques they use.

Rain by Edward Thomas

This poem was written in 1916 when Thomas was undergoing military training in preparation for fighting in World War I (WWI). He was killed in action in 1917, not long after he arrived in France. The only reference to his setting – the only detail that really locates or personalises the poem – is the 'bleak hut' in which he listens to the rain (line 2). On the face of it, the poem itself is very bleak since it focuses on lost love and the inevitability of death, but other interpretations are possible. It's a war poem that doesn't mention the war, so to an extent it universalises the experience of isolation and alienation – that feeling that there is no-one left and the end is nigh.

The story of the poem

It is midnight and the rain falls relentlessly on the speaker's hut. There is nothing but rain, solitude and his certainty that he will die. When he does die, he reflects, he won't be able to hear the rain or thank it for making him the cleanest he has been since he found himself so alone. He thinks those who have died are lucky. He prays that no-one he used to love is either dying tonight or listening to the rain awake and alone, either in pain or thinking sympathetically but helplessly about the living and the dead. Thinking in this way feels like he is a body of cold water pushing through a thick bed of stiff, broken reeds. He hopes those he once loved don't share his feeling that the rain has dissolved all his love, leaving only a love for death which is absolutely inevitable.

Form and structure

The poem is written as a single stanza with no defined rhyme scheme. The lines are mostly iambic pentameter (10 syllables with an unstressed/stressed alternating rhythm). It could be argued that the slightly monotonous rhythm reflects the relentless fall of the rain drumming on the roof of the hut. It could also be argued that the poem as a whole reads rather like a Shakespearean soliloquy. Shakespeare wrote his plays in blank verse (unrhymed iambic pentameter) and his central characters frequently soliloquise – holding the stage and addressing their thoughts to the audience as they meditate about issues relating to the rich experience of human life, or the prospect of death.

Having said there is no defined rhyme scheme, that's not to say there is no rhyme. But the rhymes are either very scattered like 'me' (line 2) and 'sympathy' (line 11), half-rhymes like 'been' (line 5) and 'reeds' (line 13), internal rhymes like 'rain', 'pain' (line 11), 'again' (line 3), or the result of repetition – 'rain' (lines 1, 10, 15). You could refer to these collectively as echoes of rhyme which feel incomplete and unsatisfactory, reflecting the melancholy tone of the poem.

Language features

- Repetition - 'rain' features three times in the first line and eight times in the poem as a whole, if you include one use of it as a verb 'rains' in line 7. Particularly in the first line, this feels relentless and mirrors the reality of the unending rain – it just keeps on coming. The word 'solitude' is also repeated (lines 2 and 6) and there is a cluster of death words – 'die' (line 3), 'dead' (line 7), 'dying' (line 9), 'dead' (line 12), 'death' (line 16). Again, the feeling of something relentless and inevitable is produced by this repetition. There is, it seems, a deliberate decision not to vary the vocabulary. Even the adjective 'wild' is used twice to describe the rain (lines 1 and 15). This adds to the feeling of resignation. However, the poem ends with two examples of more imaginative language.
- Simile - following the above idea, there is only one simile when Thomas offers the idea that lying listening to the rain is 'Like a cold water among broken reeds,/Myriads of broken reeds all still and stiff' (lines 13-14). Inspired perhaps by the rain, Thomas's simile suggests the coldness of death and a sluggish, heavy movement – a struggle, the feeling of being trapped or of moving through dead bodies on the way to death himself. So 'broken reed' could be seen as a metaphor for a dead body. The more you look at this simile, the more chilling it becomes – a nightmare image anticipating the WWI battlefields strewn with the dead and dying.
- Personification - briefly, in the final line, the rain is referred to as a 'tempest' which 'tells' Thomas that death is coming. It's a haunting final image in a poem that leaves us feeling death has come to claim Thomas. Doubtless, this was the feeling shared by many men on the point of embarking for the war.

Style focus: Rain, rain and more rain

The rain in Thomas's poem is relentless and monotonous, shown through the repetition and the iambic rhythm. Setting the poem at 'midnight' adds a layer of gloom to the misery suggested by the weather. Twice, the rain is described as 'wild' and at the end of the poem it is a 'tempest' that speaks to him. All this is slightly at odds with the idea Thomas puts forward that the rain has been 'washing me cleaner' (line 5). Although this could be literal, he isn't actually on the battlefield at the time of writing, but in military training, so a metaphorical reading is possible: the rain is purifying or cleansing him – but of what? Later he says it has 'dissolved' all his loves (line16) – it has metaphorically prepared him for death by cleansing him of any residual human feelings of love. It has made him ready to leave, to die. What's more, in the poem's only simile, Thomas sees himself as being 'Like a cold water' (line 13). In some way, he has become like the rain and slightly dehumanised, awaiting only death. Rhyming 'rain', 'pain' and 'again' – a painful elongated assonance of 'ai' - means there can be no doubt, ultimately, that the rain is a negative force.

Themes and ideas

- Death - Thomas presents death as inevitable – 'I shall die' (line 3) – but also as something to be welcomed as he says 'Blessed are the dead' (line 7), because they no longer 'hear the rain' (line 4), suggesting that death is the end to human misery. In fact, as the poem goes on, he suggests that he loves death – the rain has dissolved, diluted or washed away all his human relationships, leaving him ready and waiting for death, loving only death because it is inevitable and 'Cannot...disappoint' (line 18). He describes death as 'perfect' (line 17) which may seem odd, but which reflects how far his solitude has taken him: he can no longer imagine living, he has already entered the world of the dead 'Like a cold water among broken reeds' (line 13) and he is completely (perfectly, wholly) resigned to dying.
- Solitude - this is linked to the 'bleak hut' in line 2 and repeated when he speaks about being 'born into this solitude' (line 6). Although Thomas suffered frequent bouts of depression, he did have a wife, children and many good friends. This particular solitude is the result of enlisting in the army, and exploring the metaphor in line 6 suggests that he viewed this as a second birth. In other words, he is already acknowledging the death of his former life; now, in his isolation and alienation, cut off from people, he awaits physical death. As such, he inhabits a kind of twilight or liminal existence 'Helpless among the living and the dead' (line 12). Sharing this thought on paper in the form of the poem reinforces this sense of isolation.
- Love - this is not a love poem, and you can't imagine Thomas's wife being thrilled to read it since love of humans is all in the past tense – 'none whom once I loved' (line 8). He now has 'no love...except the love of death' (lines 15-16). He's not certain this is love – 'If love it be' (line 17), but it is all he has.

Tone

Sombre, melancholic, morbid, resigned, bleak and *depressed* seem appropriate words to describe Thomas's tone. You might also argue that there is an element of *self-pity,* although he is outward-looking enough to hope that no-one else feels as miserable as he does! There is a *matter-of-fact* quality to his resignation, his acceptance that death is inevitable. When he acknowledges that the rain has washed him cleaner than he has been for some time (lines 5-6) you could argue he is being *ironic*.

Talking points

Death is presented as inevitable, but do you find the poem entirely pessimistic? If not, pick out the elements of the poem that suggest something other than pessimism.

Does the lack of detail about setting make the poem more or less vivid to you? Think about it.

Practice Questions

How does Thomas create strong feelings about death in *Rain*?

How does Thomas make *Rain* such a powerful expression of human emotions?

Wider reading and extension tasks for interested students

The Soldier by Rupert Brooke was written at a very similar time when the poets are facing the prospect of death. Compare their ideas about death, the way they use natural imagery and the tone of the two poems.

The Road Not Taken by Robert Frost was inspired by walks he enjoyed with Edward Thomas. He wrote it for Thomas who was undecided whether he should enlist for WWI or not. It's thought that the poem encouraged him to do so. Read Frost's poem before re-reading *Rain*. To what extent do you see any regret in Thomas's poem?

Killed in Action (Edward Thomas) by W H Davies was written after Thomas died in 1917. Reading this and *The Road Not Taken* by Robert Frost, it is clear that Thomas, a married man with children, was a much-loved friend. Knowing this, how do you respond to Thomas's idea that he 'loved' in the past but now has 'no love' that the rain 'has not dissolved'?

Shakespearean soliloquies mediating on life and death, such as *Macbeth* Act 5 Scene 5 'Tomorrow and tomorrow and tomorrow' or *Hamlet* Act 3 Scene 1 'To be or not to be'.

The Spirit is too Blunt an Instrument by Anne Stevenson

This somewhat awkwardly titled poem is about the wonder of the human body and the apparent impossibility that such an intricate and amazing biological creation could have anything to do with the human spirit, what Stevenson refers to as 'the vagaries of the mind'. The poem contrasts body and spirit but ends slightly inconclusively because the speaker doesn't resolve the reality of the connection between the two. The reader is left with quite a lot of work to do!

The story of the poem

The speaker repeats the title and asserts that the 'spirit is too blunt an instrument/to have made this baby'. The words 'this baby' create a scenario, or a narrative, where the speaker is perhaps looking at their own newborn child or grandchild. However, this narrative isn't developed in any way: we don't know any objective details about the speaker or the child. Having made the opening assertion, this is effectively repeated: 'Nothing so unskilful as human passions/could have managed the intricate/exacting particulars'. The remainder of the stanza lists some of the intricacies of the human form – tiny bones, tendons, nerves and vertebrae. The speaker instructs the reader/auditor to look at eyelashes, fingernails, ears, and to imagine what is beneath: tiny blood vessels, nerves and connections. The speaker then challenges the auditor to name any human emotion that has any such precision. Without waiting for a reply, the speaker denies that is possible for human passions (the spirit) to have anything to do with such perfect automatic biological processes – 'the body's ignorant precision'. What the human spirit does is to 'invent/love and despair and anxiety/and their pain'.

Form and structure

The poem comprises three irregular and unrhymed nine-line stanzas. Its structure comes from the content. *Stanza one* asserts a position (a repetition of the title) and then attempts to back it up. *Stanza two* includes two imperatives ('Observe' and 'Imagine'), directing the reader to consider further evidence. *Stanza three* is a challenge followed by a rapid reassertion of the opening position. The final three lines are a sad corollary to the idea of the body's perfection – it is our minds that produce the pain of love, despair and anxiety. This quite logical form feels in keeping with the speaker's focus on scientific processes; she offers a proof for her proposition. However, the ending feels very inconclusive – reinforced by that final very short line. Something isn't quite resolved here: perhaps it is the paradox that although we don't control the biological processes involved in creation, love – one of the aspects of the human spirit that Stevenson mentions – is often fundamental to initiating pregnancy.

Proportionally, much more of the poem is given over to celebration of the body, but we should always note where a poem ends – the speaker's final thought is negative about the human spirit and its capacity for creating pain.

Emjambment is used effectively at various points in all three stanzas to create pace – as the words tumble from one line to the next there is a distinct sense of the speaker's energy and conviction. Lists are used in stanzas one and two with the same effect.

Language features

- Lexical set – the body: the language used to describe the biological processes involved in creation is precise, scientific, elevated and complex with lots of reference to small size: 'intricate...exacting...tiny...resilient...ganglia...fine...difficult' (stanza one); 'distinct...sharp...complexity...concentric...miniature....minute...infinitesimal capillaries...flawless...neural filaments' (stanza two); 'perfectly...precision' (stanza three). The cumulative effect of this is to suggest something elevated and significant. It also helps to create a sense of the speaker's awe.
- Lexical set – the spirit: by contrast, the lexis used to describe the spirit – the human emotions, 'mind' or 'passions' – is pejorative: 'blunt...unskilful' (stanza one); 'vagaries' (stanza three) – meaning erratic changes. The suggestion is that human emotions are messy, awkward, clumsy and uncertain. These two lexical sets are in *juxtaposition*, so the effect of one is enhanced by the other. In comparison to logical, unthinking biological processes, human emotions are not straightforward or 'possessed of the simplest accuracy' (stanza three).
- Metaphor - 'the chain of the difficult spine' (stanza one) is a lovely metaphor for the interconnecting bones, discs and tendons that protect the spinal cord. It evokes something more mechanical than organic.
- Syndetic listing - in the final two lines, the syndetic listing of 'love and despair and anxiety/and their pain' feels heavy, as though the speaker is tired of the burden of these messy human emotions.

Themes and ideas

- Creation and biology - the speaker is full of awe, amazed at the wonder of the complex human body.
- Self-destruction - the idea that in our minds we 'invent....pain' is difficult to accept. As readers we are left with an incomplete idea at the end of the poem. We have the capacity for 'love' but also for 'despair and anxiety'. In other words, we have the capacity to spoil what biology has rendered so perfect.

Tone

The speaker's tone is both *celebratory* and *judgemental*; she is full of *awe* and *wonder*, but also of *frustration* and *cynicism*. Overall, she sounds confident that she is right: our basic biology is good but somehow we manage to mess things up!

Talking points

Do you think the poet's celebration of new life is marred by her negative judgements about humans and their emotions?

Practice Questions

How does Stevenson write powerfully about the human body in *The Spirit is too Blunt an Instrument*?

How does Stevenson create a sense of beauty and wonder in *The Spirit is too Blunt an Instrument*?

Wider reading and extension tasks for interested students

Born Yesterday by Philip Larkin. Compare Stevenson's complex, scientific lexis to the way Larkin uses natural imagery to describe the baby body. Explore the way in which both poets contrast body and spirit as parts of being human.

Prayer Before Birth by Louis MacNeice is written from the perspective of an unborn child facing the horror of being born into a world of pain. To what extent is MacNeice's vision of humanity a hyperbolic extension of Stevenson's 'love and despair and anxiety/and … pain'?

Child by Sylvia Plath. Plath contrasts the eye of the child – 'the one absolutely beautiful thing' with her own image reflected in that eye – 'this dark/Ceiling without a star'. Read *Child* and then re-read Stevenson's poem: does doing this make you feel more or less positive about Stevenson's ideas?

From *Long Distance* by Tony Harrison

Often referred to as *Long Distance II*, this poem is part of a large collection called *The School of Eloquence,* published around 1981. *Long Distance I* is written in the voice of Harrison's father, complaining about life after the death of his wife. *Long Distance II* picks up the story: the mother has been dead for two years, but the father is in denial. His way of coping with grief is to continue his caring habits and pretend the wife is still there. He tries to hide this from his atheist son who believes 'life ends with death, and that is all'. Ironically, by the end of the poem, when the father is dead as well, the speaker recognises he has inherited some of this desire to remain connected as he calls his father's disconnected phone.

The title may refer to this phone call as being a 'long distance' call – a distance in time and space – and, simultaneously, to the emotional distance between father and son whilst the former was alive and the latter was unable to connect to his father's belief that the mother had 'just popped out to get the tea'. Ironically, it is only when there is a long distance between them in terms of death that the son closes that emotional distance and reproduces some of his father's behaviours.

The story of the poem

The speaker's mother has been dead for two years but his father still warms her slippers by the gas fire, puts hot water bottles on her side of the bed and renews her bus pass. The speaker says you can't just drop in, you have to phone to give him notice: he wants an hour to put away all her things which he's got out, because he realises people are going to judge him for this exhibition of his 'still raw love'. He doesn't want to risk the speaker's attitude to death tainting the way he thinks about his wife; in his own mind he is certain that he will hear her key in the lock, that she has just popped out for some tea. The speaker then gives us his view: life ends with death. Dead people haven't just gone shopping. However, revealing that his father has now died, he acknowledges that he has his father's disconnected telephone number in his new phone book – and that he still calls.

Form and structure

The poem is written in four quatrains, following the form of a *stretched* or *Meredithian sonnet*. This 16 line version of the sonnet form was used by the 19th century poet George Meredith in his long sonnet sequence *Modern Love*, with its themes of failed marriage, adultery and death. Meredith uses an abba cddc effe ghhg rhyme scheme where the final stanza offers a summary or presents a turning point. Harrison plays with this slightly: the first three stanzas are abab alternating rhymes, but he switches to ghhg for the final stanza, indicating a shift in direction. This shift is an unexpected twist: having rejected his father's way of grieving as nonsense – 'I believe life ends with death, and that is all' - the focus shifts to the speaker and the revelation that he is still phoning his now dead father's disconnected number. So, the shift in rhyme scheme indicates a shift in *tone* (stoical acceptance to poignant pining?), in *focus* (father to son) and in *content* (rejection of denial as a way to cope with grief to recognition that he does the same).

The regular rhyme and frequent enjambment make this a very easy-to-read poem; it feels conversational – particularly in stanza two when Harrison almost invites us into the conversation saying 'You couldn't just drop in. You had to phone.'

Language features

- First person pronouns – the first person speaker uses first person pronouns very minimally – only the possessives 'my mother' and 'my blight of disbelief' in the first three stanzas. This makes the end-stopped declarative at the start of the final stanza very emphatic and dramatic: 'I believe life ends with death, and that is all.' That stanza begins and ends with the only first person subject pronouns (those with verbs attached) – 'I believe' and 'I still call'. Those two phrases sum up the paradox of the poem: there is a contradiction between his actions and what he believes. His action in calling defies the logic of his belief, but speaks to an essential human impulse to retain some connection with those we have loved. It's also worth noting that Harrison doesn't use first person when he says 'there's your name' in the phone book; in practice, he means *I wrote your name and number in the phone book* but omitting the subject pronoun and verb implies the name somehow just found itself in the book, as though it's a surprise to him. The more you think about it, the more clever this is: he's denying the instinct that made him write out his father's name and number, just as he is in denial about his father's departure.
- Second person pronouns – these are used in stanza two to draw in the reader: 'You couldn't just drop in. You had to phone./He'd put you off'. What he means is 'I couldn't just drop in' but he depersonalises it so that the reader feels included in the scenario. In the final stanza, use of second person pronouns is quite different: he is addressing his dead father – 'You haven't both gone shopping...your name'. The placement of 'I believe' above 'You haven't' on the page emphasises the contradiction discussed above. As soon as he asserts his belief, he undermines it by speaking as if his father were listening. At the same time, if 'you' is his father, we are now excluded from the poem and left in the position of eavesdroppers; this makes the final stanza even more poignant.
- Metaphor – 'my blight of disbelief' is worth unpacking. Blight is a disease that makes plants wither. By extension, it's something that destroys. So the speaker says his father won't risk the son's disbelief (in the continuing presence of the mother) spoiling the way he thinks and feels about his wife.

Themes and ideas

- Love, death and grief – love in this poem is endless and endures in the face of death. The father's actions are all the result of his 'still raw love' (stanza two). 'Raw' is normally a word used of grief, so Harrison gives it a new energy and resonance by applying it in a slightly surprising way to love. When food is raw it is fresh, uncooked; when a wound is raw it is painful; when an emotion is raw it is strong, intense, powerful. The father's 'raw love' is all these things – it is unfinished, painful and intense; his grief isn't over. He exhibits love through his sweet, attentive, caring gestures and by surrounding himself with 'her things'. These actions are irrational, and we could view him as deluded but the fact he clears things away before visitors come shows he is fully aware of how he will be judged – he is not deluded at all; these acts are a choice resulting from his continuing love and the rawness of his grief. What's interesting is that he feels obliged to 'look alone' (stanza two). This suggests that his method of coping with loss – denying it – protects him from the loneliness that normally accompanies such bereavement. Nevertheless, he is grieving and that grief is endless – he's always waiting for the key in the lock that will 'end his grief' (stanza three). We could say that the message of the poem is that grief does strange things to people – as the speaker finds himself calling his dead father's 'disconnected number' – but it seems more about the reality that we can't and shouldn't judge the way people cope with bereavement until we've felt such loss ourselves. Denial is normalised.
- Time – the only thing that changes with time in this poem is the speaker's attitude. Love, grief, habits (such as warming slippers and making phone calls) remain.
- Faith – the poem advances a distinct contrast between the father's confidence and faith in his wife's return – he is 'sure' and 'He knew' – and the speaker's atheism – his 'blight of disbelief' (stanza three) and his belief that 'life ends with death, and that is all' (stanza four).

Tone

The tone throughout could be described as *matter of fact* but it is possible to read into those first three stanzas a few notes of *embarrassment, frustration* or *mockery*. Beginning 'Though my mother was already two years dead' suggests he is perhaps embarrassed by his sentimental father. The frustration comes through in those two short declaratives and the way he engages the reader in the situation in stanza two – 'You couldn't just drop in. You had to phone.'. Mockery could be seen in the italicisation of 'He *knew*' in stanza three. He might be described as *sarcastic* as he refers to his own 'blight of disbelief', or you could see this as *self-deprecating*. At the end, his *confident* assertion of what he believes and his declarative 'You haven't both gone shopping' is totally undermined by what is almost a note of *surprise* – 'there's your name....I still call'.

Talking points

How do you feel about the way Harrison writes about his mother? She is 'mother' and so little described that she occupies very little space in the poem. On the other hand, his father is 'Dad' and is the focus of three whole stanzas. The speaker is able to believe 'life ends with death, and that is all' after his mother's death. After his father's death, however, he transfers a disconnected number to the new phone book and makes calls.

Practice Questions

How does Harrison make *Long Distance* such a poignant poem?

Explore the way Harrison writes movingly about grief in *Long Distance*.

Wider reading and extension tasks for interested students

Material by Ros Barber and *Effects* by Alan Jenkins are two early 21st century poems written following the death of a mother. Compare their ideas about the way people cope with the death of an elderly parent.

Funeral Blues by W H Auden

Written in the 1930s but popularised in the late twentieth century through its use in the film *Four Weddings and a Funeral*, this hugely popular poem seems to sum up very poignantly the intense grief of bereavement – a grief which makes you feel the whole world should stop and take notice. It's strange to discover, then, that it started out as something quite different. It was written as part of a play and was really a rather sarcastic, comic piece. Originally five stanzas, the final three were cut and replaced by two new stanzas and it is these which swing the whole poem in a different, more serious and more poignant direction. Look closely, though, and it is possible to see glimpses of the original comedy in the first two stanzas (see Hyperbole and comic images under Language features, below).

The poem was also used as a cabaret song before it was published – hence the title 'Blues' in reference to blues music. It could also refer, of course, to depression which is known colloquially as the blues, although such an informal term as 'blues' rather underplays the seriousness of bereavement's effects. Interestingly, Auden didn't really settle on a single title for the poem: it is sometimes called *Stop All the Clocks*. The poem as we have it today was published in 1938, not long before the start of World War II. Like much of Auden's poetry, it reflects some of the disillusionment of those inter-war years: 'I thought that love would last for ever: I was wrong' and 'nothing now can ever come to any good'.

The story of the poem

The speaker issues a series of commands which are all about creating silence – no ticking clocks, no phones, no barking dogs, no pianos. Even the drum for the funeral should be muffled as the coffin and mourners come. What's more, he wants aeroplanes to fly over, using their smoke trails to write a message on the sky: 'He is Dead'. He wants 'crepe bows' tied around the necks of pigeons and for policemen to wear black gloves – signs of respect for the dead. The dead man was everything to the speaker – a compass giving him direction – and he filled all parts of his life – work, leisure, day, night. The speaker thought love would last forever but now realises he was wrong. He asks for the stars to be put out, the moon to be packed away, the sun to be dismantled, the ocean to be poured away and the wood to be swept up. Nothing good can happen any more.

Form and structure

The poem can be described as an elegy – a lament for the dead. The 16 lines of the poem are organised into *rhyming couplets* within four quatrains. The rhythm is slightly disjointed, with 9-12 syllable lines and no discernible pattern. The strong rhyme makes it easy to overlook this lack of regular rhythm, but it makes the poem slightly jerky and uneven. This is compounded by the use of several *end-stopped lines*. There's a sense that the intense emotion is disrupting an even flow of thoughts. Where the poet uses *enjambment* in stanza one, there is a strong sense of the speaker's emotion spilling over as he visualises the funeral procession: 'with muffled drum/Bring out the coffin'.

As described above, this poem has been revised several times. One revision, presumably made to secure the rhyme, was in the penultimate line; the original 'sweep up the woods' became 'sweep up the wood' in order to create a full rhyme with 'good'. 'Woods' makes more sense of course, being a large element in nature in line with stars, moon, sun, oceans. 'Wood' feels a bit odd in comparison.

Stanzas one, two and four are almost exclusively lists of imperatives – outward-looking, addressing an unspecified reader or audience, telling them they should be mourning, that the world should be mourning, that they should shut down everything. When you look at the commands you see a progression from the local and achievable (stanza one – stop the clocks, cut off the phone, shut up the dog, stop playing the piano, bring out the coffin) to the increasingly surreal (stanza two – get planes to write on the sky, put bows on pigeons, all policemen to wear black gloves) and impossibly large-scale (stanza four – put out or eliminate the stars, sun, moon and oceans). So the poem is structured to show an *escalation* in demand, perhaps reflecting an increased sense of desperation on the part of the speaker.

Meanwhile, stanza three stands out as being quite different: this is the only place where the speaker uses first person pronouns, intensively exploring – again via a list – what the dead man meant to him. Returning to the escalated demands after this makes sense, doesn't it? In articulating what the death means to him, the speaker realises none of the earlier demands are enough – the whole world has to shut down.

Language features

The language of the poem is very familiar which is one reason the poem is so popular and widely used.

- Imperatives – these form the backbone of this poem with 14 in total, spread across three stanzas (12 lines). That's intense! See above (Form and Structure) for a discussion of the way these demands escalate. Nine of the imperatives appear at the start of lines.
- Hyperbole and comic images – the hyperbole reaches a pitch in the final stanza with the demands for sun, moon, stars and oceans to be eliminated. But earlier there are slightly surreal and almost comic images such as the idea of 'crepe bows round the white necks of the public doves'. 'Public doves' is probably a slightly mocking euphemism for pigeons but regardless of this, the idea is a joke. Likewise, the aeroplane 'Scribbling on the sky' evokes cartoon imagery of a plane using thick vapour trails to write words. This comedy may be a hangover from the poem's first appearance in a play (see opening comments, above).
- Alliteration – hard 'c' alliteration is seen early on with 'clocks...cut...coffin' whilst 'muffled' and 'mourners' gives us a more muted sound to match the near-silence the speaker wants to achieve. In stanza two, the 'sk' alliteration of 'scribbling on the sky' returns us to that very hard, almost savage sound.
- Repetition – 'my' is used nine times in three lines – intense repetition which emphasises the scale of the speaker's loss and how much the dead man meant to him.
- Lexis of sound – this is obvious in stanza one ('clocks...telephone...dog barking...pianos') but more subtle in stanza three ('my talk, my song') where it becomes clear that the speaker's desire to silence the world stems from the fact that his own world has been silenced – he has no talk and no song now that his loved one is dead. Notice the only sound he wants is the droning of the aeroplanes which he refers to as 'moaning'. Onomatopoeia is used in the long vowel sound here to create the sound of his grieving. 'Moaning' is also so close in sound to 'mourning' that it feels synonymous (has the same meaning).
- Imagery of light – in the final stanza, 'stars...moon...sun' represent major light sources that the speaker wants to shut down so that there is an external darkness to match his internal darkness or depression.

- Symbolism – in the above collection of lights, both 'stars' and 'moon' are typically used to represent love, whilst the 'sun' represents happiness. All of this is over for the speaker.
- Ambiguity – to 'Stop all the clocks' is to eliminate the sound of their ticking, but it also suggests a desire to stop time, as though life (all life, everything in time) should not go on since the loved one is dead.

Themes and ideas

- Grief – the power of grief to isolate and to consume a person is clearly evoked in the poem which also explores the idea that private grief sometimes isn't enough. The speaker wants the whole world to stop and share his sense of loss. It is the impossibility of this which reveals the speaker's isolation so poignantly. You could argue that the hyperbolic and slightly ridiculous demands the speaker makes show how irrational he has become in his grief.
- Death – the above is relevant to this theme, of course, but notice the way death brings disillusionment: 'I thought that love would last for ever: I was wrong'. This is a beautifully, although brutally, constructed line. The romance and idealism is cut off with that *midline caesura* – the colon – and devastatingly reversed with the assertion 'I was wrong'. Death doesn't just take away life, it robs us of our idealism and hope.

Tone

The speaker is in a state of *despair, frustrated* at the indifference of the world. He sounds *distraught, defeated* and *disillusioned* in stanza three. At the end of the poem he seems *depressed*.

Talking points

How do you feel about the rather comic images in the poem – the dog with his juicy bone, the doves with their crepe bows, the aeroplane scribbling, the moon being packed up – and so on? Is this hyperbole an effective expression of grief or does it undermine the seriousness of the poem?

Would you prefer to read 'woods' or 'wood' in that penultimate line? Is it better to secure the rhyme or the sense?

Practice Questions

Explore the ways in which Auden makes *Funeral Blues* so moving for you.

How does Auden make *Funeral Blues* such a powerful expression of grief?

Wider reading and extension tasks for interested students

Time does not bring relief: you all have lied by Edna St Vincent Millay is a sonnet expressing intense grief at the continued sense of loss felt by the bereaved speaker. Compare the way she and Auden use hyperbole and references to nature.

He Never Expected Much by Thomas Hardy

Subtitled 'A Consideration On My Eighty-Sixth Birthday', it's probably safe to see this as an autobiographical poem and to refer to Hardy and the speaker as being the same. The poem was not published until Hardy died about two years later, in 1928. Hardy was a prolific writer who published about 1,000 poems as well as 14 novels and many short stories. His novels are notoriously bleak as well as beautiful and poignant, particularly the last – *Jude the Obscure*; it was because this novel attracted so much negative comment that he stopped writing fiction and focused on poetry. The poetry is serious stuff too, however! In some ways, this poem can be seen as a bright and breezy attempt to show he is reconciled with life's unfairness, so it is, superficially at least, one of his more positive poems. Big questions remain, however, about its tone and whether Hardy is as stoical and pleased with his approach to life as might appear at first glance. Is he attempting an act of self-persuasion? The reader is left to decide.

Using the third person in the title suggests Hardy is writing his own epitaph: you can imagine it inscribed on a tombstone – *Here lies Thomas Hardy, novelist and poet. He never expected much.* Alternatively, you might think he was writing the epitaph he thought he would be given, based on his reputation. Either way, it's a rather bleak and sad insight into someone with pessimistically low expectations of life.

The story of the poem

Addressing the World (Life), the speaker says life has kept its promise and been pretty much as it said it would be. Since he was a child, lying down in the meadow looking at the sky, the speaker has never expected life to be fair. He says he was told then by the World in a mysterious voice echoing from the clouds and hills that different people have different views on life: some love it, some are chilled about it and some are cynical – until they die. The World does not promise much – just some not very exciting random happenings. The speaker thinks this was a wise warning and he took it to heart; it meant he could manage all the effort and pain of life that came his way each year.

Form and structure

The poem is in the form of a *monologue*, although the speaker recreates the voice of the World in direct speech in stanzas two and three. The poem is addressed to the World – to Life, really. You could refer to it as having elements of an imagined dialogue recalled from the past when the speaker was a child. You can also use the term *apostrophe* for this kind of poem. An apostrophe is an address to a subject not literally present eg God, Fate, Destiny.

There are three very regular stanzas with an aaabcccb rhyme scheme and an 84868886 syllable count. Hardy was known for his use of tight forms – he was not an experimental poet, unlike his fellow poets of the 1920s such as T S Eliot. Hardy's forms are a hangover from the nineteenth century. Having said that, it is possible to see meaning in this form – a monotony and predictability which fits with the ideas of the poem. Some people find the repetition in each stanza's line 2 to have a song-like quality. Others see it as a bored sigh, reflecting the repetitive grind of life. This repetition – for example 'kept faith with me,/Kept faith with me' in stanza one – can be referred to as *epizeuxis*.

Language features

- Casual and qualifying language – beginning 'Well' and continuing with qualifying phrases such as 'Upon the whole' and 'I own', the poem has a very conversational and slightly vague feeling which adds to the tone of resignation.
- Images of nature – although you wouldn't say this is a poem about nature, there are references such as 'I used to lie/Upon the leaze and watch the sky' and 'that mysterious voice you shed/From clouds and hills around'. These are undecorated images with no adjectival detail, and yet they feel significant. In stanza one, we feel this should have been a positive experience – relaxing in the meadow, watching the sky with all its connotations of space, hope and possibility. And yet the speaker is not able to see any of this; he is uninspired by nature. Likewise, in stanza two, he presents clouds and hills as enclosing or blocking. The voice he hears is 'mysterious' and

yet he is not curious. So the lack of imagery is significant in revealing his rather limited imagination.

- Verbs – there are relatively few relating to the speaker, so worth noting that in stanza one both 'lie' and 'watch' suggest his passivity. He doesn't seem like a get up and go person, does he?
- Colour symbolism – the speaker refers to 'neutral-tinted haps'. This basically means grey – a non-colour – and is full of symbolic value. The World promises nothing more than this – a bleak, colourless, boring existence.

Themes and ideas

- Stoicism – this refers to enduring difficulties and pain without complaining. Hardy seems stoical in this poem – he never expected that 'life would all be fair' and this patient, resigned approach has enabled him to plod along, to 'stem such strain and ache/As each year might assign'.

Tone

The tone is very *flat, resigned* and slightly *dejected*. There is a *frank, honest* quality to the speaker's voice and you could describe him as *stoical*. But perhaps there is also a slightly *rueful* or *wistful* note? Whether this amounts to regret is debatable. He is slightly *melancholic* (gloomy) and cuts a rather isolated figure, with no references to any other humans in his life. It is possible to read his line in stanza three 'Which I for one failed not to take' as slightly *smug*, as if he's saying well *I* didn't get caught out by life. Ironically, of course, the reader suspects that he has been caught out – he's lowered his expectations so much that he hasn't been able to see or seize any of life's opportunities. Realism has become pessimism.

Talking points

Is Hardy being ironic throughout this poem? In other words, is he saying something he doesn't mean? Try re-reading the poem with this in mind and see what you think.

Practice Questions

How does Hardy vividly convey his feelings about life in *He Never Expected Much*?

How does Hardy use words and images in *He Never Expected Much* to create such a fascinating poem?

Wider reading and extension tasks for interested students

Neutral Tones by Thomas Hardy explores the idea of 'neutral-tinted haps' in terms of a failed relationship. With literal references to 'grayish leaves', Hardy creates a neutral palate but draws out the horror of a life without colour. After reading, go back to the last stanza of *He Never Expected Much* – is Hardy's reference to 'neutral-tinted haps' subtly suggesting that the life of resignation and low expectations is actually bleak?

Far From the Madding Crowd by Thomas Hardy is a novel about the 'strain and ache' of life, which the protagonist Gabriel Oak faces with stoicism and patience. Unlike the speaker in this poem, however, (spoiler alert) he finally gets the prize. This may well be Hardy at his most optimistic!

One Art by Elizabeth Bishop is a poem laden with irony as the speaker attempts to persuade herself that it's possible to master the art of losing things, including lovers. Her façade cracks in the end. Compare the voice of Bishop's speaker with that of Hardy's poem: does the experience of reading *One Art* make you more or less convinced that Hardy is attempting to persuade himself that he did the right thing in having low expectations?

The Darkling Thrush by Thomas Hardy is typical of Hardy's gloom and clear-eyed pessimism. On the eve of a new century, against a bleak landscape, the thrush 'fling[s] his soul' with 'joy illimited' and perhaps 'Some blessed

Hope, whereof he knew/And I was unaware'. It's not happy reading, but go back to *He Never Expected Much* and compare the tone: does the bright and breezy vibe of this poem suggest the speaker is trying a bit too hard?

The Telephone Call by Fleur Adcock

On the face of it, this is a bizarre poem about a hoax phone call telling the speaker they have won the lottery – no money, just the wonderful experience of being told they've won! Beneath the comically bizarre surface, however, is a very serious allegory about the nature of human hope, our complicated attitudes towards luck, the inevitable disappointment of life and living a life at the whim of our emotions. Winning the lottery is a fantasy, a dream which takes us away from the humdrum nature of everyday life. Adcock's poem takes the fantasy – and therefore the disappointment – to another level. Viewed like this, the actions of Universal Lotteries are cruel and perhaps reflect a dark sadistic side to human behaviour.

Originally from New Zealand, Fleur Adcock is a contemporary poet whose work frequently has this kind of a dark twist. This poem was first published in 1986 but has probably gained in relevance in the UK since the introduction of the National Lottery in 1994. Even without this context, however, winning the lottery is a common metaphor for good fortune, for surprise good luck, which strengthens the idea of an allegorical reading.

The story of the poem

The speaker is in conversation with someone from Universal Lotteries. They ask if she is sitting down and then tell her she's won a top prize of over a million pounds – what would she do with it? They check she's still there and prompt her to talk about her feelings. The speaker initially says she can't believe it. More prompting and the speaker describes feeling intense emotions, like the top of her head has floated out of the window. More prompting and the speaker describes physical symptoms – she might be going to sneeze or cry. The caller encourages the speaker to given in to these emotions and have a little cry. Then the speaker says she hasn't bought a lottery ticket for years. The caller laughs and reassures her – they are operating a special lottery for everyone who has ever bought a lottery ticket; they select someone at random. The speaker still can't quite believe it but says she will when she sees the cheque. Then it is revealed there is no cheque, no money; all they are offering is the experience of being told you have won – that's the prize. They say 'Have a nice day' and the phone goes dead.

Form and structure

The poem is written in the form of an anecdote – a short story. We are plunged *in media res* into a telephone conversation. The whole poem is in dialogue apart from two phrases: 'And they laughed' (stanza one) and 'And the line went dead' (stanza six). There is no rhyme – the whole poem is written in free verse, although divided into six eight-line stanzas. The poem is structured so that the final stanza offers a twist and an anti-climax.

Language features

- Lexis of universality – words like 'Universal' and 'Global' in stanza one and phrases such as 'That's what they all say' (stanza two) and 'Nearly everyone's bought a ticket' (stanza five) suggest this is about a universal, shared human experience of hope and disappointment.
- Imagery – the imagery describing sensation in stanza two is quite extreme. The speaker says 'I feel the top of my head/has floated off, out through the window,/revolving like a flying saucer', combining a metaphor and a simile in an extravagant idea. You could say this represents a

disconnect between logic and hope: in order to focus on the giddy experience of hope, the speaker has to detach brain from body and stop thinking logically. The caller's insistence on getting the speaker to articulate this feeling has produced this intense response from someone who previously said 'I can't believe it'. The caller is exploiting the speaker, forcing the articulation of emotions.

- Imperatives – the caller insists 'tell us' (stanza two), repeats 'Go on' (stanzas two and three), and gives other instructions: 'don't be ashamed' (stanza three), 'Relax...have a little cry' (stanza four) and finally, ironically, 'Have a nice day!' (stanza six). The caller orchestrates the call, ensuring the speaker is fully invested in the idea of winning, perhaps to increase the disappointment.
- Questions – these are used to secure the speaker's engagement in the process and, at the end, to mock: 'You've had a great experience, right?/Exciting? Something you'll remember?'. The mocking feels stronger because the questions come thick and fast and the speaker has no chance to reply.
- Ambiguity – the poem's final word 'dead' relates to the telephone line but might be hinting at the death of hope for the speaker.

Themes and ideas

- Hope – the poem sets out a bleak vision of human hope as leading to inevitable disappointment. The speaker is initially guarded – 'I just...I can't believe it!' but allows herself to indulge – hence the anti-climax is stronger. The idea seems to be that human experience always fall short. Life – represented in the form of the caller from Universal Lotteries – is a hoax that promises a lot but fails to deliver.
- Greed and materialism - you could read the poem's allegory as a warning against greed. When we indulge our fantasies we are demonstrating dissatisfaction with what we have.

Tone

The speaker's tone is initially one of *disbelief,* then *excitement* and some *cautious scepticism*. The caller's tone is more consistently *enthusiastic, encouraging* and *confident*. In the final stanza it's more difficult to judge – is there cruel *mockery* and *sarcasm*?

Talking points

Does the fantastical nature of this scenario detract from your appreciation of the point Adcock may be making about life?

Is Adcock cynical? Or do you think she displays sensitivity and understanding of the way humans live their lives?

Practice Questions

How does Adcock create a sense of hope in *The Telephone Call*?

How does Adcock make *The Telephone Call* such a powerful expression of hope and disappointment?

How does Adcock vividly convey ideas about life in *The Telephone Call?*

Wider reading and extension tasks for interested students

Please Hold by Ciaran O'Driscoll is a similarly comic but serious poem that tells the story of the speaker's telephone conversation with a 'robot' at the bank. What do these two poems have in common in terms of the way they represent modern life?

A Consumer's Report by Peter Porter

Published in 1970, this poem from Australian poet Peter Porter explores the meaning and experience of life using an absurd parody of a consumer feedback survey, as though *Life* was a product. Although the premise is ridiculous, the poem presents a new way to think about human life and an opportunity to pause and reflect on our belief systems, the way we are using the time we have, and what we are getting out of life.

The speaker gives a mostly unfavourable review, with some heavy criticism. Through the extended metaphor of *Life* as a product, it's suggested that it is boring, expensive, flawed and confusing. At the end, however, a final judgement is reserved until the alternative can be tried. Since the only alternative to life is death, or perhaps the afterlife, the poem ends with an irony which redirects us to think about human complacency and arrogance. The poem as a whole offers a critique of our consumer society and the way things are commodified – turned into a product.

The story of the poem

The speaker states he has tested a product called *Life*, has completed the form he was sent and understands that his answers are confidential. He had *Life* as a gift. He didn't feel much when using it and would have liked to be more excited by it. It seemed soft but left behind embarrassing excretions. It wasn't particularly good value and he has used up more than he thought – he has about half left although it's difficult to tell. There are lots of instructions and they contradict themselves so it's difficult to know which to follow. The speaker isn't sure the product should be given to children. He struggles to think *Life* has a purpose; one of his friends said it was just to keep the maker in a job. He wonders whether we actually need *Life* now, since things are piling up and the world managed without *Life* for a thousand million years. He observes that Life seems to come in lots of labels, sizes and colours when it should be more uniform. The shape is awkward, and although it's waterproof, it's not heat-resistant; it doesn't last but it's hard to get rid of it. It can be cheapened if not so much is put into it and sometimes you get it even when you don't ask for it. The speaker agrees it's a popular product – people say they're on the side of *Life* – but he thinks it's over-rated, just a small thing that makes people behave badly. It's nothing special – we should take it for granted. Life's experts, he says, might be called philosophers, market researchers or historians but consumers are the ones who count. He'd buy the product, but he reserves judgement about whether it's a best buy until he receives the alternative product he's been promised.

Form and structure

NOTE: the poem as printed in the official CIE Songs of Ourselves anthology appears to be missing two lines (after line 19 'It's difficult to think of a purpose'). This analysis is based on the 51 line poem seen elsewhere. To avoid confusion, however, line numbers have not been used when referring to particular quotes in the second half of the poem.

The poem has 51 lines across 2 stanzas – a three line prologue that sets up the premise of a consumer feedback survey, and a 48 line stanza which contains the feedback itself. Although there is reference to a 'form' in line 2, the report is very conversational and sounds like a dramatic monologue, addressed to a silent and anonymous auditor – 'you' in the second line, presumably God. The use of free verse adds to the conversational feel of the poem. But the writer maintains the illusion that a form is being completed with the short, almost epigrammatic, points which read as though they are short responses to a series of printed questions.

Language features

- Extended metaphor – the whole poem can be described as an extended metaphor whereby life is compared to a consumer product.
- Lexis of consumerism – the language of consumerism is repurposed very effectively and humorously, including the legalese of 'I...understand that my answers are confidential' (line 3) and words such as 'economical' (line 9), 'instructions' (line 13), 'purpose' (line 19), and later 'price', 'respondent', 'labels', 'uniform', 'waterproof', 'heat resistant', 'cheaper', 'delivered', 'product', 'consumers', 'best buy' and 'competitive product'. This lexis has nothing to do with life or the human body, but Porter is very skilful in creating a disturbing connection which forces us as readers to reconsider our attitudes.
- Lexis of products – linked to the above, terms like 'waterproof' and 'heat resistant' create humour when applied to the human body.
- Euphemism – the 'embarrassing deposit' of line 8 could be a reference to excrement or, more obliquely, to memories. Further on, 'Things' could be referring to people so that 'Things are piling up so fast' is a comment on over-population. Seen in this light, the preceding line 'the price is much too high' could be seen as eco-critical: human beings are costing too much in terms of damage to the environment. These euphemisms capture the essence of the poem: comic yet serious. More sombre, perhaps, is the idea that 'it's very difficult to get rid of', a dark reference to committing suicide, and the idea of a 'competitive product' – a euphemism for death or the after-life.
- Word play – Porter plays very cleverly with some phrases that people use in relation to life. For example, the idea that life is made cheap, a phrase which suggests people don't value or have devalued life. This becomes 'whenever they make it cheaper they seem/to put less in' which is ironic – of course, it's what a manufacturer would do, but how does that translate to human experience? We cheapen life if we don't invest in it, if we don't put more into the business of existing. Similarly, 'people/even say they're on the side of it' is a play on the idea of being on the side of life, meaning embracing life and all its opportunities. These word plays create irony and humour, but also pose a question about the way we as humans use the life we've been given.
- Negatives and qualifiers – 'didn't' (line 5), 'but' (line 8), 'It was not' (line 9), 'but' (line 12), 'although' (line 13), 'I don't know' (line 15), 'I'm not sure' (line 17), and later 'I don't like', 'but not', 'it doesn't', 'yet'. All these expressions have a dampening effect on the poem, contributing to the sense of disappointment and disillusionment.

Themes and ideas

- The Body – with its 'awkward' shape and its mixed bag of qualities, being 'waterproof' but not 'heat resistant', the human body is largely criticised in the poem. It doesn't present the kind of uniformity that consumers demand of their products these days and seems burdensome. Porter uses a technique called defamiliarisation here – making us view something familiar in a different way so it that it becomes strange. It's unsettling to view the human body as a commodity isn't it?
- Existentialism – this is a philosophical enquiry which explores the issue of human existence. The speaker asks the question very directly when he says 'It's difficult to think of a purpose/for it', but the poem as a whole challenges us to consider the value we place on life and the way we treat the human body.
- Disappointment and dissatisfaction – life hasn't excited the speaker and there are lots of negative expressions and qualifying statements.

Tone

The tone can be described as *mock-serious*, *sarcastic* or *tongue-in-cheek*. The speaker is *confident* and *assertive* in offering opinions, but seems *jaded*, showing some *negativity*, *disappointment* and *dissatisfaction*. You could also use the word *reserved* or *downbeat* – the speaker is apparently *unemotional*.

Talking points

Is the poem funny, thought-provoking about the value we place on human life, or a dark satire on consumerism? If you were told the poem was amusing before you read it, would it make a difference to your judgement?

Practice Questions

How does Porter use words and images to striking effect in *A Consumer's Report*?

How does Porter use words and images in *A Consumer's Report* to create such a fascinating poem?

Wider reading and extension tasks for interested students

Do Not Go Gentle into that Good Night by Dylan Thomas offers a very contrasting perspective on life, creating an urgency about staying alive. After reading the Thomas poem, how would you describe *A Consumer's Report*? Does it seem cool or cold? Which poem do you prefer?

Request To A Year by Judith Wright

In many ways, this is a remarkable poem and an interesting observation on the centuries-old female struggle against the weight of social expectation. Published in 1955, it is an autobiographical account based on the diaries of Wright's great-great-grandmother and a sketch passed down through the family. So we can refer to the speaker and Wright as one and the same and infer that when Wright describes her great-great-grandmother as a 'devotee of the arts', she is in fact demonstrating a similar commitment to the arts in writing her own poetry.

The story of the poem

The speaker says that if the year is planning a gift for her she would like it to be the attitude of her great-great-grandmother who was famously devoted to the arts. This woman had eight children and very little opportunity to paint. One day she sat on a high rock beside a river in Switzerland. From a long distance she saw that her son was drifting on an ice-floe towards a high waterfall. Her quick-thinking daughter managed to get a walking stick out to him and saved him. The mother herself could do nothing so she quickly sketched the scene. The sketch survives to this day, proving the story. The speaker asks the year if it has no other Mother's day present in mind, to reach back in time and bring her the great-great-grandmother's 'firmness of hand'.

Form and structure

The poem is written in five quatrains and one rhyming couplet. Initially it reads as very conversational free verse with no rhyme and no clear rhythmical pattern. However, rhyme starts to appear in stanza three with 'ice-floe' and 'below'. This continues with 'day' and 'way' in stanza four, then becomes stronger with the half-rhyme of 'done' and 'scene' as well as the full rhyme of 'eye' and 'by' in stanza five. Stanza six is a full rhyming couplet. So you could argue that the rhyme solidifies across the course of the poem. This could reflect the poet's confidence in the actions of her great-great-grandmother, or a sense of her own poetry shaping up so that by the end she is already demonstrating that same commitment to the arts that she values in her grandmother – the same 'firmness of hand' in her own writing.

The form of the poem can be described as an *apostrophe* – an address to a subject not present or able to respond – in this case, the 'year'. The poem is structured so that the first and last stanza act as a frame; the address and the request to the year are repeated, creating a kind of circularity, framing the narrative.

Enjambment is used during the action to create pace; look particularly at the last two lines of stanza two and the way they wrap onto the first line and a half of stanza three before there is a midline caesura after 'second son'. The last two lines of this stanza are also enjambed, recreating the unchecked flow of the ice as it drifts towards the waterfall, and enhancing the drama of the narrative at this point. Having said this, the drama as a whole is quite understated, particularly when the conclusion of the story in given in parentheses as a kind of afterthought!

There is only one line in the poem which stands as a complete sentence: 'The sketch survives to prove the story by.' This makes the line stand out and gives a central importance to the artwork and its symbolic value: art can preserve a moment, a memory or – in this case, perhaps - an 'attitude'. The great-great-grandmother is not attempting to cover up what some might judge to be her lapse in maternal care. Rather she is boldly displaying her pragmatic attitude, her steadiness and her skill as an artist, whilst memorialising her daughter's heroic role.

Language features

- Personification – the year is personified as a being who allocates gifts.
- Symbolism – the 'petticoats of the day' (stanza four) would have been cumbersome garments which limited movement. The speaker says they no doubt 'impeded' the daughter. They are a clear symbol of the barriers or impediments to women achieving their potential. In this case, however, the daughter heroically pushes past the impediment and succeeds in rescuing her brother. The physical reality of the petticoats and their obvious symbolic value helps the reader to see that similar impediments are at work for the mother: gender norms and expectations of mothers will restrict her creativity if she lets them.
- Ambiguity – the 'isolating eye' of the artist (stanza five) is highlighted to the reader through the assonance, but what does it mean? One meaning could be that the artist's eye zooms in on the detail and isolates it, bringing it into sharp focus. Alternatively, it could suggest that the artist's eye is more objective, achieving an emotional distance. The final phrase 'firmness of her hand' (stanza six) is also ambiguous. Physically and literally, it refers to the great-great-grandmother's steady hand as an artist. But we know from stanza one that the speaker is in search of an 'attitude'. Emotionally, a 'firmness of … hand' could be seen as a steadiness, a calm pragmatism that isn't hysterical but suggests someone with a clear sense of what to do in a given situation. Does it also refer to her steely determination to put her art ahead of everything else at this particular moment, or to her steady refusal to take any blame for not saving the child herself?
- Parentheses – the brackets used around the final line of stanza four present the conclusion of the drama – the fact that the son is saved – as something of an afterthought. This draws attention to the fact that the focus of the poem is the great-great-grandmother and her 'attitude'; the story is just an example of that attitude, and the speaker is much more interested in the woman than the fate of her son.

- Euphemism – the great-great-grandmother is said to be at a 'difficult distance' from her son (stanza three). The word 'difficult' is a euphemism capturing the fact that the mother was far away but without any sense of judgement from the speaker. It is the distance that is difficult, and not a failing of the woman for placing herself at a distance from her children.

Themes and ideas

- Art – for some people, this is the dominant theme of the poem – the importance of art (whether painting or poetry) in memorialising or bearing witness, and the vital detachment an artist requires in order to complete important creative work. It is, after all, the sketch that 'survives to prove the story' (stanza five) and it is true that Wright's role as a poet is subtly brought into play through the increasingly solid rhyme (see Form and structure, above).
- Motherhood and women's lives – for many people, however, the poem is more about the role of women as mothers, societal expectations and gender bias. Wright exposes those expectations as a limitation on creative expression since the great-great-grandmother had 'little opportunity for painting pictures' and the story invites criticism of her for sitting 'one day' at a 'difficult distance'. The 'petticoats' of the daughter also inhibit freedom and equality of opportunity. However, the poem bears witness to the strength of women over successive generations – two in the poem (mother and daughter) and Wright herself, composing this poem. All three women have success that society might have denied them - this is what the poem implies although never directly states. Since Wright refers to 'Mother's day' in the final stanza, we can infer that she is a mother herself.
- Subversion – not only is the mother a quietly subversive figure who takes a rare moment to focus on her art rather than childcare, but there is a reversal of the normal hero-victim gender profile since it is the daughter who rescues the son. At the end of the poem we are being invited by the speaker to see the great-great-grandmother's 'firmness' or pragmatism as a valuable quality – something which is often admired in men but which may be criticised in women who are still, sometimes, expected to be more emotional or self-sacrificing. The adverb 'hastily' in stanza five is interesting – why do you think she was hasty? Does it speak to her quick-thinking and resourcefulness: knowing that she could not save her child she did all that she could to capture the moment and memorialise it? Does it suggest panic or artistic skill? You could argue that the debate over the way we view the great-great-grandmother is captured in that one well-chosen word. See Talking Points below for more discussion of this.

Tone

The speaker's tone is one of *admiration* for the great-great-grandmother. She begins in a very *formal* manner and is largely *unemotional,* perhaps reflecting some of that avoidance of sentiment that she admires in her ancestor. Alternatively, you might see a *tongue-in-cheek* humour in the poem, as Wright brings a controversial and almost fantastical scenario to us.

Talking points

What is your instinctive reaction to the bare bones of this story? An artistic woman with eight children takes a rare moment to paint but is nowhere near her children when a potentially fatal emergency arises. Danger is only averted when one of the children rescues the other. The mother's contribution is to draw the scene at a distance. Try telling the story like this to some people who haven't read the poem and get their reactions. In the third decade of the 21st century, are we still expecting women to give up everything in favour of childcare? Is our instinct to blame women when children have accidents? Do we expect women to react emotionally to danger?

To what extent to you think the poem challenges us to formulate our own reaction before we read the final couplet?

Practice Questions

How does Wright create strong feelings about women's lives in *Request To A Year*?

How does Wright vividly convey her admiration for her great-great-grandmother in *Request To A Year*?

Wider reading and extension tasks for interested students

Material by Ros Barber is a contemporary autobiographical poem in which the speaker reflects with some nostalgia on her mother's approach to parenting, contrasting it with her own. Do these female ancestors from the two poems share any qualities? How would you describe the contrasting styles of the two poems (think about form, structure, language and tone)?

Hidden Lives by Margaret Forster is an autobiographical memoir in which Forster looks back at the lives of her grandmother and mother before finally examining her own life. A talented writer of both fiction and non-fiction, Forster offers an unsentimental and clear-eyed view of women's changing lives over the twentieth century.

On Finding a Small Fly Crushed in a Book by Charles Tennyson Turner

Published in 1873, this poem is the work of a Victorian poet and priest, brother of the more famous Alfred Lord Tennyson. Charles Tennyson Turner was a prolific sonneteer, composing more than 300 sonnets with several, like this, focusing on small things like insects. This sonnet is addressed to a dead fly that has been squashed inside a book. The speaker uses this incident to reflect on the way the book of life will close on all of us in time. Victorians were frequently preoccupied with death and frequently very sentimental in their writing about it. Tennyson Turner bucks that trend, however, in this largely unsentimental, pragmatic poem.

The story of the poem

Speaking to the fly, the speaker says someone has inadvertently squashed it between the pages of a book, but notes what a lovely monument has been created, with the fly's wings spread out and gleaming, preserving its essence. He wishes that the memories we left behind were half as lovely. The fly's life was pure and blameless – he's died like a saint, shining. For humans, death is always close at hand and we live with the prospect day by day. The book of life will close on us, perhaps just as we get up one day in summer. Unlike the fly, however, we won't leave any shine or glory behind.

Form and structure

The poem is a sonnet – 14 lines of 10 syllables, with a defined rhyme scheme – abba cddc efef gg. Sonnets will often divide into an octet (lines 1-8) and a sestet (lines 9-14), with a volta or pivot. In this case, the volta comes at the midpoint of line 8 where the poet switches his attention from the dead fly to humans and their impending, inevitable death: 'Now thou art gone: Our doom is ever near'. The midline caesura marks the pivot. The rhyming couplet that finishes off the poem is suitably pithy and rather gloomy: 'The closing book may stop our vital breath,/Yet leave no lustre on our page of death.' Sonnets are typically thought of as love poems but they are used more widely to capture a thought or idea – a little song or sound, which is what *sonnet* means in Italian or Latin. The full rhymes used throughout give a note of confidence to the poem which link to the meaning: the speaker has a clear-sighted and pragmatic view of human life and death.

You could also describe the form of the poem as an *apostrophe* – an address to a subject not present or able to respond.

Language features

- Hyperbole – there is some exaggeration around the beauty of the fly which is, after all, just a squashed insect. Words and phrases such as 'fair' (line 3), 'gleam' (line 4), 'lovely' (line 6), 'pure', 'blameless', 'shine' (line 7) pick up the natural iridescence of the insect's wings and extrapolate this to suggest a saintly character for the fly. The word 'relics' (line 7) contributes to this, since relics of saints are preserved in Catholic tradition.
- Extended metaphor or conceit – the metaphor of the book of life closing is extended through the sonnet: 'the book will close upon us' (line 10) and 'The closing book' (line 13) obviously refer to the moment of inevitable death, and the metaphor also contains the idea that we all have 'our page of death' (line 14), picking up on a Biblical idea from Revelation 20 v 12 'another book was opened, which is the book of life. And the dead were judged by what was written in the books, according to what they had done'. No doubt the priest Tennyson Turner was familiar with this passage.
- Contrasting lexical sets – the beauty of the dead fly (see lexical set in Hyperbole, above) is contrasted to the negative lexis used about humans – 'doom' (line 8), 'peril' (line 9), 'no lustre' (line 14).

Themes and ideas

- Mortality – death is presented as close at hand, a daily fear, inevitable and unpredictable. The poet even suggests it might come at a particularly pleasant moment – 'Just as we lift ourselves to soar away/ Upon the summer-airs', picking up subtly on the comparison to the fly which was no doubt about to take off when the book was closed, crushing it. Life is as fragile as a bug. The idea that we will 'leave no lustre' behind is hard to stomach, however. It suggests humans cannot expect a legacy with any value. As a priest, perhaps Tennyson Turner was trying to encourage the reader to stay humble, but also to reflect on whether our actions are having any lasting impact.
- Memory – the idea that a fly's memorial or 'monument' is more valuable than a human's legacy is tough but clearly stated: 'Oh! that the memories, which survive us here,/Were half as lovely as these wings of thine!'. The more times you read the poem, the more it feels like a warning to humans: be realistic about who you are and strive to make the most of your time on earth.

Tone

The speaker is *tender, gentle, respectful* and full of *admiration* in the way he speaks to the fly. Throughout, there is a *thoughtful* tone, with hints of *sadness* and perhaps *regret* or *resignation* as he talks about the inevitability of death and his sense that we will not leave behind anything beautiful as a memorial. The sadness is not overdone, however, and the tone remains largely *unsentimental*.

Talking points

How successful is Tennyson Turner in prompting the reader to consider their attitude to life? Which are the phrases which have most impact?

Practice Questions

Explore the ways in which Charles Tennyson Turner makes *On Finding a Small Fly Crushed in a Book* so moving for you.

How does Charles Tennyson Turner use words and images in *On Finding a Small Fly Crushed in a Book* to create such a fascinating poem?

Wider reading and extension tasks for interested students

The Flea by John Donne is a poem that also uses an insect to make a point about human life. Compare the tone of the two poems and the way the poets develop a central *conceit* (idea) through their extended metaphors. Make a case that Charles Tennyson Turner did or did not have Donne's poem in mind when he wrote his sonnet.

Ozymandias by Percy Bysshe Shelley

This poem was written in 1817 and published in 1818 as a response to the news that remnants of a huge statue were being brought from Egypt to the British Museum. Shelley and his friend Horace Smith challenged each other to write a sonnet to mark the occasion. The head and torso remnants came from a statue of Rameses II, an Egyptian pharaoh from the thirteenth century BC, who built numerous monuments and temples – memorials that he thought would give him some kind of immortality. It's thought that Shelley hadn't seen the statue when he wrote the poem. He based some of his ideas on the writing of a Greek historian, Diodorus Siculus, who described a statue and the words inscribed on it: 'King of Kings Ozymandias am I. If any want to know how great I am and where I lie, let him outdo me in my work'. Ozymandias is the Greek name for Rameses.

Written two years after Napoleon was defeated at Waterloo and thought by many to be an allegory for Napoleon's failed attempt to impose his dictatorship on Europe, this poem continues to resonate. For example, in 2003 the dictator Saddam Hussein, who had erected hundreds of monuments to himself and engaged in a massive building programme, was overthrown and a gigantic statue of him in Baghdad was pulled down. *How are the mighty fallen* would be a good subtitle for the poem.

The story of the poem

The speaker says he met a traveller from an ancient land who told him a story. The story is about the remnants of a huge statue seen in the desert: two legs without a body; a frowning face with sneering, hard features inscribed on it; and a pedestal (a statue base or plinth) with an inscription. He says the sculptor did a good job re-creating in stone the character of Ozymandias, a cruel dictator who mocked his people. The inscription reads 'My name is Ozymandias, king of kings:/Look on my works, ye Mighty, and despair!' The speaker then turns his attention to the desert and notes that there is 'Nothing' there; around the wreckage of the huge statue the sands stretch far away into the distance, with no buildings and no end in sight.

Form and structure

The poem is written in the form of a sonnet – the form chosen by Shelley and Smith for their competition. However, since the sonnet is traditionally used for love poetry, you could argue that the sonnet form mocks Ozymandias's self-love. It's also worth noting that Shelley ignores the convention of an octet/sestet structure (8 lines followed by 6 lines, often with a volta or turning point at the start of the sestet). Instead, his traveller-speaker rushes on with the story – line 9 begins 'And'. The volta, when it comes, is seen in the juxtaposition of lines 11 and 12: 'Look on my works, ye Mighty, and despair!'/Nothing beside remains'. The irony and sense of anti-climax is possibly the most striking feature of the poem. Shelley also ignores the convention that there should be no crossover rhymes between the octet and the sestet. Instead, he rhymes lines 7 and 10 ('things' and 'kings'). So, Shelley defies the conventions of the sonnet – hardly surprising from a radical, anti-authoritarian Romantic poet writing about the deluded and corrupt ways of an authority figure!

The poem is structured with three voices, creating a layered effect and an increasing sense of distance. It starts with the first person speaker saying 'I met a traveller from an antique land'. The traveller then speaks, describing the statue and quoting the third voice, that of Ozymandias in the form of words inscribed on his statue: 'My name is Ozymandias...' The poem then reverts to the traveller's voice describing the desert. The sense of distance in both time and space creates a sense of myth and mystery which adds to the fable-like quality of the poem.

The layering is also seen in the way Shelley gradually reveals details of Ozymandias, the sculptor, the people and the landscape.

Shelley's *Ozymandias* is structured so that we are left at the end staring out into the desert. Shelley doesn't offer overt judgement or suggest how we should respond. It's interesting to compare Smith's sonnet (see Wider Reading, below) which brings us right back to London and our own lives, perhaps challenging our complacency by suggesting in the future someone might look at the remains of London and wonder 'What powerful but unrecorded race/Once dwelt in that annihilated place'.

Language features

- Synecdoche – Ozymandias is referred to as 'The hand that mocked them' and 'the heart that fed' (line 8). Both of these are examples of synecdoche, where the part represents the whole. Representing Ozymandias as 'hand' suggests, perhaps, that he was physically violent and that he mocked the powerless by striking them. Interpreting the synecdoche of 'heart' is more tricky. Is it a metaphor suggesting that he survived on a diet of their misery? A kinder interpretation would suggest that he felt warmth towards his people and fed them well. That seems harder to accept, however, and it doesn't sit well with the picture of Ozymandias as proud, arrogant and cruel.
- Lexical field of size – 'vast' and 'colossal' (line 2 and 13) refer to the statue while 'boundless' (line 13) refers to the desert. The desert wins.
- Imagery of decay – 'trunkless' (line 2) creates a comic image, while 'shattered' and 'wreck' (line 4 and 13) suggest the power of nature in acting against the statue. Interestingly, the image of shipwreck is evoked twice with 'Half sunk' in line 4 and 'colossal wreck' in line 13; Ozymandias is like a wrecked ship in the desert, stranded and useless.
- Imperatives – there is a double imperative in the inscription with 'Look' and 'despair' (line 11), so Ozymandias is portrayed as commanding. It's worth noting as well that these are commands are addressed to 'ye Mighty', as though he wouldn't bother addressing ordinary people, and he refers to himself as 'king of kings' – the best of the best.
- Alliteration – the desert is described with two alliterative pairs as 'boundless and bare' and 'lone and level' (line 14). The alliteration here draws attention and ensures that the reader has a clear focus on the desert at the end of the poem. Earlier, Shelley uses hard 'c' alliteration in 'cold command' (line 5), with the hard sound suggesting the cruelty of Ozymandias. Subtly, this sound is picked up across the poem – look for the 'k' in 'trunkless', 'sunk', 'wrinkled', 'mocked', 'king of kings', 'Look', 'works' and the 'c' of 'colossal'.

Themes and ideas

- The sublime – the Romantic poets wrote about the way nature was so powerful that it inspired awe, wonder, and a feeling of being overwhelmed. That's the sublime. It's that feeling you get when you realise the insignificance of humans: compared to the natural world we are short-lived and impotent. Shelley's final lines make it clear that the natural world survives and is 'boundless', while man's 'works' decay and disappear.

- Power – above all else, the poem presents the idea that human power – perhaps political power particularly – is ephemeral. In other words, it will pass. Ironically, it is the work of the talented sculptor that has partially survived, not Ozymandias's 'works'. Real power lies with time and nature (see below).

- Time – the poem suggests that humans are insignificant in the grand scheme of things. Time moves on inexorably and our achievements will vanish.

- Arrogance, pride and vanity – the poem presents a clear picture of human failure. Despite our pride in our own achievements and our arrogance in feeling invincible, people in power are deluded. Time and the natural world will erode our power base and 'level' us all. It is ironic that the 'Mighty' addressed by Ozymandias, will 'despair' – not because of his works which outclass theirs, but because like him their time in power is brief and they will become like dust in the desert, 'level' with the least powerful person.

- Nature – from the very first line, nature is presented as eternal. The story is set in 'an antique land' and the desert is 'boundless'. It has absorbed Ozymandias's 'works' and is revealed as the most powerful force. The adjectives 'bare' and 'lone' emphasise the lack of human presence. Nature doesn't need us.

- Art – ironically, although the statue is in a state of decay, Shelley's poem has survived and continues to speak to people across the centuries, proving the power and permanence of poetry as an art form.

Tone

As discussed above, the speaker creates distance between himself and the events of the poem by ascribing the words to a 'traveller'. You could say the speaker's tone is *detached*; any judgement is left to the reader. The traveller's tone is similarly *objective* – at least on the surface. But the juxtaposition of his reading of the epitaph and the phrase 'Nothing beside remains' suggests if not confusion, then perhaps a slight *puzzlement*: where are these 'works'? Alternatively, you might argue that the traveller is *mocking* at this point. The tone of the final lines describing the desert might be described as *awed* – the traveller is in awe of the expanse of the desert and its capacity to reabsorb the puny efforts of mankind.

Talking points

How do you respond to Shelley's ideas of the sublime (see Themes, above)? Do you think these ideas about the power and longevity of nature are compromised now by our understanding of the way humans in fact do have a huge – a hugely negative – impact on the natural world?

Is Shelley promoting the power of art in the form of sculpture and poetry?

There are some tricky bits in the poem. How do you interpret the synecdoche of 'the heart that fed' (line 8)? Does it sit oddly, in your mind, alongside 'The hand that mocked them', or can you find a reading that reconciles the two?

Does it matter that Shelley re-wrote the inscription he read about?

Practice Questions

How does Shelley create strong feelings about power in *Ozymandias*?

How does Shelley use words and images in *Ozymandias* to create such a fascinating poem?

Wider reading and extension tasks for interested students

Frankenstein by Mary Shelley is a novel that explores one man's attempt to defy time and achieve a kind of immortality. Frankenstein says that he hoped 'a new species would bless me as its creator and source'. What parallels can you draw between the ideas in the novel and the poem written by Mary Shelley's husband?

Ozymandias by Horace Smith. Smith later retitled his poem: *On A Stupendous Leg of Granite, Discovered Standing by Itself in the Deserts of Egypt, with the Inscription Inserted Below*. Not a snappy title! Explore the similarities and the differences between the two poems. Why do you think Shelley's survived when Smith's is scarcely known? Which do you prefer?

The Convergence of the Twain by Thomas Hardy was used in the memorial service for victims of the Titanic sinking in 1912. Rather than concentrating on the victims, however, Hardy describes how human vanity and pride – in the form of *Titanic* – collides with nature in the form of the iceberg. Which poem, in your opinion, is a stronger condemnation of human ambition?

Sonnet 18 by William Shakespeare, one of the most famous of his 154 sonnets, ends with the idea that poetry confers a kind of immortality on the subject: 'So long as men can breathe or eyes can see,/So long lives this, and this gives life to thee.' In your opinion, does Shelley's poem give immortality to Ozymandias, to Shelley himself or to an idea about human frailty?

Away, Melancholy by Stevie Smith

Stevie Smith was a prolific poet and novelist of the mid-twentieth century. This particular poem was published in her 1957 collection, *Not Waving but Drowning*. The title poem of this collection is worth reading – it's probably Smith's most well-known poem and it provides a good counterpoint to *Away, Melancholy* (see Wider reading, below), perhaps supporting the idea that this poem is about someone doing their best to be positive rather than necessarily achieving positivity. In other words, the speaker in this poem is trying really hard to make an argument for life, for pushing away those gloomy feelings (melancholy) and focusing on what is good about being human. It could be subtitled 'Reasons to be Cheerful'. It's up to you to decide whether she has convinced herself – or you.

The story of the poem

The speaker tells herself to let go of melancholy, to cast it aside. She asks rhetorically, aren't the trees and the earth green? Doesn't the wind blow? Don't the fires leap and the rivers flow? Nature is full of energy and activity and functionality. Go away, melancholy. She notes that the ant is busy and in fact all things are hurrying to eat or be eaten. Go away, melancholy. Man hurries too – eats, has sex, dies – he is an animal too. Oh well, go away, melancholy; let it go. Man is a superior creature, though, as he is the only creature to create something to worship or aspire towards; he pours into this all his goodness and calls it God. Go away, melancholy; let it go. The speaker then turns to an imaginary devil's advocate and says don't talk to me about horrible things – tears, tyrants, plagues, wars. Don't challenge the existence or goodness of a God who can allow this. Instead, focus on the good, marvel at how good people can be. Go away, melancholy; let it go. Man aspires to be good and to love. Yes, he sighs and could give up but doesn't; even when beaten, corrupted or dying in his own blood he heaves himself up and cries 'Love'. This incredible reality is what we should be focusing on, not man's failures. Go away, melancholy; let it go.

Form and structure

The poem is written in free verse, spread unevenly across 10 stanzas. There is some rhyme scattered in places – for example, in stanza two 'blow' and 'flow', in stanza three 'busy', 'hurry', 'melancholy' as well as 'meat', 'eat'. In stanza four we see 'hurries' and 'buries' alongside 'also' and 'let it go'. We could interpret these scattered rhymes as glimmers of positivity – they suggest a speaker who can see good things but isn't completely comfortable or confident.

In terms of structure, the first and last stanzas are repetition of the lines used liberally throughout as a kind of mantra. These two stanzas form a frame for the rest of the poem, enclosing it in this address to both melancholy ('Away, melancholy') and the self ('let it go'). Anaphora is used in both these stanzas, emphasising the command 'Away'.

Within the frame, the poem is structured in five parts: the example of nature (stanzas two and three), the comparison to mankind (stanza four), exploration of man's difference in creating an ideal (stanza five), an argument with a devil's advocate or her interior voice (stanza six) and a conclusion, reaffirming what is good about mankind (stanzas seven to nine). Interestingly, stanzas seven to nine are all a combination of negative and positives which suggest the speaker is really grappling with the balance at the end, really getting into the argument. For example, in the short stanza eight, man aspires to good and to love but also 'Sighs'. However, the fact that the refrain 'Away melancholy' is heard only once in this section of three stanzas, compared to six times in the preceding stanzas, might suggest she needs fewer reminders as she gets into her stride.

Language features

- Imagery – the imagery of nature in stanza two is full of energy and positivity. Green is symbolic of new life and there is a lot of movement in the verbs 'blow', 'leap' and 'flow'.
- Triples and lists – the triple of 'Eats, couples, buries' (stanza four) creates speed and suggests a busyness to match that of the ant, but is also rather reductive in its summary of human life: we eat, we make love and we die. The list of 'tears,/Tyranny, pox, wars' (stanza six) is heavy and bleak, but neatly sums up the world's problems – misery, poor leadership, disease and conflict. In some ways, you could argue, the neat list makes the devil's advocate position seem clichéd and more easily dismissed.
- Musicality – the refrain 'Away, melancholy' is quite lyrical and feels a little like a song from a Shakespearean comedy. This is compounded with the interjection of the very Shakespearean 'hey ho' in stanza four: 'With a hey ho melancholy'. Not only does the 'ho' give another rhyme with the line endings either side ('also' and 'go'), but it feels very light and whimsical.
- Parentheses – in stanza five, parentheses are used twice around the refrain 'Away melancholy' which makes it read more as an aside. It feels as though the speaker is having a side conversation with melancholy as she tries to get on with her argument.
- Metaphor – the 'stone' of stanzas five to seven is a complex metaphor. The suggestion is that mankind raises up a stone, invests it with an idea of goodness and then calls it God. This makes sense when you think about the way primitive religions sometimes relied on physical icons providing a focus for human worship. So the stone in the poem is a metaphor for faith, for an ideal of goodness. What is interesting is the way Smith sees this as man-made, a tribute to man's goodness. The first mention of 'god' uses lower case and has to be read as referring to mankind:

'Into the stone, the god/Pours what he knows of good/Calling, good, God'. There is a play around good/God which cements the idea that the two are synonymous to Smith: it is this goodness in humans that separates us from the ants and other animals.

Themes and ideas

- Nature – nature is presented as beautiful, purposeful and active. There is a sense of resilience in nature – the ant just keeps going. Nature is initially inspiring (stanza two) but starts to become a little depressing as a model when the speaker notes that 'All things hurry/To be eaten or eat' (stanza three) which suggests there is nothing more to life than a struggle for survival. It is this that prompts the speaker to move on to more spiritual matters such as goodness and love which, it is implied, are unique to mankind, distinguishing us from animals – 'He of all creatures alone/Raiseth a stone' (stanza four). Nature is not referred to after stanza three.
- Faith, goodness and love – the references to God in the poem could be seen as referring to religion as something that sustains humans and helps them to ward off melancholy. However, the metaphor of the stone is not that specific and there is no direct mention of faith or religion. It is implied, however, that faith in mankind's ability to love and to do good should be able to sustain us, to make us keep going when we feel melancholy. When the speaker imagines the struggling man in stanza nine she says he 'heaves up an eye above/Cries, Love, love'. The word 'above' could be seen to signify looking up to the heavens, but equally he could be looking to a higher principle, something above the dross and struggle of everyday survival. The first capitalisation of Love suggests an appeal to Love as a spiritual entity; the second use with lower case could be an imperative – a command to everyone to love.
- Hope and despair – the poem, as suggested above, could be subtitled 'Reasons to be Cheerful', and it certainly could be seen as inspiring hope with its presentation of mankind's essential goodness and capacity to love. Yet there are lingering notes of despair such as the 'Sighs' single word line at the end of stanza eight and the constant refrain of 'Away melancholy' which persists to the end as though the melancholy hasn't, in fact, gone away.
- Resilience – this, it seems, is our ultimate weapon against melancholy. In the penultimate stanza, the speaker presents the 'Beaten, corrupted, dying' man who still has an instinct to look up and to refocus on love. What stanzas six to nine suggest is that we cannot deny the 'tears/Tyranny, pox, wars', and all this will cause us 'Sighs'; our 'failing' (stanza nine) isn't surprising. But we can choose to focus on something better; mankind's capacity for 'virtue' is astonishing – it 'needs explaining' because it is so amazing.

Tone

This is debatable and you might usefully experiment reading the poem in different styles to see which you find most convincing. You could argue that the speaker is *determined* and *energised*, *reasonable*, *logical* and *rational*. You could also see notes of *desperation* at times, particularly since she has to repeat 'Away, melancholy' and 'let it go' so frequently!

Talking points

Do you find the poem beautiful and uplifting? Or is it slightly desperate?

To what extent are you convinced by Smith's argument relating to humanity's superlative status in being able to raise up a stone (create an idea of God/good)?

Practice Questions

How does Stevie Smith movingly convey ideas about human life in *Away Melancholy*?

How does Stevie Smith make *Away Melancholy* such a powerful expression of hope and despair?

Wider reading and extension tasks for interested students

Not Waving but Drowning by Stevie Smith is another of her poems that focuses on someone suffering from melancholy or despair. Compare the voice of *Away, Melancholy* with the voice of the drowning person. What would one say to the other?

Ode on Melancholy by John Keats implores the reader not to give in to melancholy. Compare the solutions offered by the two poets.

Exam Information: Paper 1 Poetry and Prose

Section A: Poetry component (one 45 minute essay) is worth 25% of your overall IGCSE.

There is a choice of two questions – each will focus on ONE poem and the poem will be printed for you. You do not take your annotated poems into the exam.

Assessment Criteria

There are four specific Assessment Objectives (Aos).

AO1 Show detailed knowledge of the content of literary texts in the three main forms (drama, poetry and prose), supported by reference to the text.

AO2 Understand the meanings of literary texts and their contexts, and explore texts beyond surface meanings to show deeper awareness of ideas and attitudes.

AO3 Recognise and appreciate ways in which writers use language, structure and form to create and shape meanings and effects.

AO4 Communicate a sensitive and informed personal response to literary texts.

All AOs are equally weighted, which means you have to keep all of them in mind. What this means in practice is that you should:

• show clear knowledge of the poems, refer to details and use well-selected quotations

• demonstrate clear understanding of themes and ideas – the deeper implications of the text

• respond sensitively and in detail to the way the writers achieve their effects

• make a perceptive, convincing and personal response.

Exam Question Styles

Explore the ways in which the poet makes this poem so moving for you.

How does the poet movingly convey (a theme) in this poem?

Explore the ways in which the poet uses powerful words and images.

Explore how the poet powerfully conveys (a theme or idea).

How does the poet use words and images to striking effect?

How does the poet create strong feelings about (a topic)?

How does the poet make this poem such a powerful expression of (an emotion)?

Exam Tips

- Break down the question – be clear that you will have to address WHAT and HOW (the content and the way the poem has been written) – the question should direct you to a theme (eg loss) and/or focus you on style (eg powerfully presents/vividly creates).
- Plan – make sure your plan has clear points about the theme so that you can show your understanding of the poem's content.
- Support all your points with quotation – multiple quotation if possible.
- Stylistic and language comment should accompany the quotation.
- Explore effects – the impact on the reader or the different interpretations that might be possible.
- Create paragraphs that have the following shape:
  POINT – responding to the question focus
  EVIDENCE - quotation
  DISCUSSION – effect/interpretation and reference to technique
  Your teacher may have an alternative version of this PED structure – be guided by your teacher.

Glossary

Alliteration: the term used to describe a series of words next to or near to each other, which all begin with the same sound. This creates particular sound effects eg *a hairy hand, the luscious leaves.*

Ambiguity (noun), **ambiguous** (adjective): (from the Latin for 'doubtful, shifting') the capacity of words and sentences to have double, multiple or uncertain meanings. A **pun** is the simplest form of ambiguity, where a single word is used with two sharply different meanings, usually for comic effect. Ambiguity may also arise from **syntax** (when it is difficult to disentangle the grammar of a sentence to resolve a single meaning), and from **tone** (where the reader cannot tell, for example, whether a given text is to be read seriously or not).

Anaphora: repetition of a sequence of words at the beginning of consecutive lines.

Apostrophe: an address to a subject not literally present eg God, Fate, Destiny.

Association or **Connotation:** a word can suggest a range of associations and connections in addition to its straightforward dictionary meaning. For example, *heart* has many associations with love, courage and other human values, besides its literal, biological meaning.

Assonance: the repetition of identical or similar vowel sounds in neighbouring words. It is distinct from rhyme in that the consonants differ while the vowels match eg *Shark, breathing beneath the sea/Has no belief, commits no treason.*

Cacophony: a harsh, discordant mixture of sounds.

Caesura: (plural caesurae) a pause within a line, marked by punctuation.

Conceit: an elaborate and unlikely comparison between two things that is developed to make a point. An extended metaphor.

Emotive language: language that provokes a strong emotional response.

Enjambment: where lines of poetry are not stopped at the end, either by sense or punctuation, and run over into the next line. The completion of the phrase, clause or sentence is held over.

Epizeuxis: the immediate repetition of a word or phrase eg in *Macbeth,* 'O horror, horror, horror!'

Euphemism: (from the Greek for 'speaking fair') unpleasant, embarrassing or frightening facts or words can be concealed behind a euphemism: a word or phrase that is less blunt, rude or frightening than a direct naming of the fact or word might be. Hence 'to kick the bucket' is a euphemism for death; 'would you like to wash your hands?' is a polite euphemism for the question 'would you like to urinate?' Sexual functions, death and body parts are typically disguised in this way in common speech.

Euphony: a collection of harmonious, pleasant sounds; the opposite of **cacophony**.

Explicit: something which is stated directly and made very clear; the opposite of **implicit**.

Hyperbole: (from the Greek for 'throwing too far') emphasis by exaggeration.

Imagery: words used to create a picture or sensation, through **metaphor, simile** or other figurative language. Usually **visual** imagery - something seen in the mind's eye – but also
auditory imagery - represents a sound
ol**factory** imagery - a smell
gustatory imagery - a taste
tactile imagery - touch, for example hardness, softness, wetness, heat, cold.

Implicit: something which is implied, or which can be inferred, but which is not explicitly stated; the opposite of **explicit**.

In media res: beginning in the middle of the action.

Irony: (from the Greek for 'dissembling') irony consists of saying one thing when you mean another. Irony is achieved through understatement, concealment and allusion, rather than by direct statement.

Metaphor: the most widespread figure of speech. In metaphor, one thing is compared to another without using the linking words like or as, so it is more direct than a simile. One thing is actually said to be the other eg *My brother is a pig. The man is an ass.* Verbs can also be used metaphorically: *love blossoms.* Metaphors create new ways of looking at familiar objects and are also commonly found in everyday speech eg *the root of the problem.*

Motif: a recurring idea, image or theme.

Narrative: story.

Narrative viewpoint: there are two main narrative viewpoints. In a **first person narrative**, the narrator is a character in the story who retells his or her first hand account of events. In a **third person narrative**, the narrative voice stands outside the story and is not a character. This type of narrative voice tends to be more objective and often is omniscient (that is, all-seeing) and able to show the reader the thoughts of all the characters.

Onomatopoeia: where words sound like the things they describe eg *hiss, crash, murmur, creak*.

Oxymoron: a figure of speech that combines two contradictory terms eg *bitter sweet, living death, wise fool*.

Paradox: (from the Greek for 'beside-opinion') an apparently self contradictory statement, or a statement that seems in conflict with logic or opinion. Lying behind this superficial absurdity, however, is a meaning or a truth.

Persona: a character created by the poet.

Personification: a form of figurative language in which animals, inanimate objects and abstract ideas are addressed or described as if they were human eg *The breeze whispered gently. The trees waved their tops.*

Power words: words that have a powerful effect in a text.

Sibilance: the recurrence of sounds known as sibilants which hiss - *s, sh, zh, c, ch* – eg *Ships that pass in the night, and speak each other in passing.*

Simile: in a simile, one thing is compared to another using the linking words *like* or *as* eg *as big as a giant; he smoked like a chimney.*

Symbol/symbolism: a symbol is a person, place, or thing that comes to represent an abstract idea or concept -- it is anything that stands for something beyond itself. Symbols are often universally understood eg green = jealousy; poppy = remembrance; cross = sacrifice. Linked to **metaphor** but not quite the same – a metaphor is more consciously creative and original.

Synecdoche: part of something is substituted for the whole eg *all hands on deck* where sailors are referred to as hands.

Zoomorphism: non-animal objects, people or situations are given animal attributes.

Printed in Great Britain
by Amazon

33135133R00029